T0147481

oOh My Testicles!

oOh My Testicles!

A tale of entanglement

Lyndon Baptiste

iUniverse, Inc.
New York   Bloomington

iUniverse books may be ordered through booksellers or by contacting:

iUniverse
1663 Liberty Drive
Bloomington, IN 47403
www.iuniverse.com
1-800-Authors (1-800-288-4677)

Because of the dynamic nature of the Internet, any Web addresses or
links contained in this book may have changed since publication and may
no longer be valid. The views expressed in this work are solely those of
the author and do not necessarily reflect the views of the publisher, and
the publisher hereby disclaims any responsibility for them.

ISBN: 978-1-4401-4989-4 (sc)
ISBN: 978-1-4401-4990-0 (ebook)

Printed in the United States of America

iUniverse rev. date: 06/02/2009

Lyndon Baptiste was born in 1982 and lives in Trinidad and Tobago. He is a software engineer, lecturer and novelist who, thank goodness, writes for the fun of it. He is the author of *90 Days of Violence* and *Boy Days.*

To you valiant doctors and nurses who nurture your patients before your pockets.

AUTHOR'S NOTE

I write this with mild bewilderment and amusement for while I can coolly avert jests, traditionally some words and phrases are simply taboo, and should they ever be uttered, one risks chuckles, giggles, absurd remarks or being looked at askance. Ironically, however, I know that I am not the first, and certainly not the last, man to suffer some testicular ordeal. Hence, I present you with *oOh My Testicles!*

Written ages ago, I chose not to edit this story. Firstly, for the fear of astute dictums through language holding preponderance over emotional trauma; this feature story was written within two weeks, while I recovered at home, therefore it is a part of my life which I hold dear, even in its raw, crude form. To morph it *now* is to lose the essence of what happened *then*.

Special thanks to Lance and Louise Baptiste. And to Aunt Sylvia who visited me despite her terminal illness, a memory which will *hopefully* never fade. And to the family and friends who supported me. And to the doctors and nurses at Port of Spain General who pampered and cared for me as a son; your service and dedication are priceless.

oOh My Testicles!

<<<<<<<<<<<<<<<<<<<<<<<<<<<<<<<<<<<<<<<<<<<<

I stood, hands on hips, gauging the handiwork of a job which could have been finished in hours but was now in its second, tedious week. The bedroom was a small, airtight furnace with four walls of rough concrete slabs coated with splashes of vibrant orange and yellow, yet an impasto of the previous green, once a source of easy flattery, still peeked out mockingly. Brushes, rollers, tins, cloth, cardboard and blotches of paint were scattered everywhere, the latter across the dusty grey tiles, on top of the cupboard and on my arms and face. Mumbling, I tested the ladder's sturdiness with light bounces on the first rung and, with a languid nod, purposed that the task would be completed before the new bed and executive tempered glass desk arrived at dawn. Renewed, but still muttering angrily, I scurried up the step ladder and leaned my two hundred pound frame carelessly against the top cap.

Without warning, a searing pain struck. My goodness, what was it? It was neither my stomach nor appendix, but my testicles. No… it was only *a* testicle, my right ball to be precise. I became stunned and only through divine intervention regained my balance, but not my composure, and with wild gesticulations, six feet above ground level, I grasped the ladder. I still do not believe that being either shot or knifed is as painful as the pangs which, like little red devils armed with electric pitchforks, stabbed the areas around and through my groin. Given man's proclivity to intently guard his genitals, I hastened to cup my source of dismay, movements which catapulted the tin of paint off the ladder's platform to the woe of the tiles which became a brilliant sea of orange. A more urgent matter had surfaced and I wobbled away from my duties to my parents' bed which, sadly, was empty.

The ramifications of *critical* illness are phenomenal for it is as crucial as death, engaging as marriage, and as lonely as a graveyard. Even the sluggard struck by a pandemic is forced to adopt science, diet or philosophy. I had on one occasion even heard of an ascetic atheist who wept bitterly that God would lighten his burden when death was at his doorstep. Subject to such conditions, man has the capacity to change, and I did that night, although I must admit only temporarily, and without hesitation I will go as far as wagering that a man would more readily agree to lose a finger, maybe even both hands and legs, to save his manhood, because the penis, like the vagina, remains the single gateway to sinful pleasure, matrimonial joy and procreation.

I am neither proficient with medical terms nor homeopathy, but as I lay besieged by soreness, I concluded that there wasn't a single identifiable incident where I had heard a male complain about a testicle; it was always their *jewels* at risk. I lay discomforted and spent a sleepless night careened on my left. When the sun peeked inside, I telephoned Roxanne to take me to the doctor and, no, this couldn't wait until later.

To my pleasure, we arrived at the general practitioner's office at seven-thirty sharp but this joy was short-lived as Dr. Narine was the best and cheapest in town; even though both gates to the establishment were closed, there was already a host of pallid, reticent folk lined against the borders of the compound and staring inside with blank, watery eyes as if beyond the shut, brown door was life itself. At the entrance was a pony-tailed, red-skinned chap who was conspicuous not only because of his height but also because he was slouched over the gate in agony, his legs spread apart, holding a handful of crotch. Maybe he had a *ball* problem too, I thought.

At seven-forty-five on the dot, a giant of a man barged out of the office, locked the brown door behind him, and without a word to the anxious patients, snapped open a heavy-duty lock, and almost flung the main gate open. While he fussed over the side entry, the sick filtered in disorderly and manned the free locations closest to the entrance. Interspersed among the huddle, Roxanne explained to me that each morning, except on Sunday, Dr. Narine's son opened the gates at the exact hour, and for a brief moment, forgetting that she had a toddler in tow, I became worried that, perhaps, my cousin was not as well as she appeared – how else would she know this? Without warning, my testicular pain struck and I impatiently unsettled the crowd with hurried excuses, and in the southwestern corner of the courtyard I sat on a weather-beaten concrete bench which joined another at an acute angle and was shaded by a gaudy metal shed.

I don't know whether minutes or hours passed but I must have dosed off because, when my eyes opened, there were about a dozen people sitting with me. Roxanne was to my left, her backside halfway off the bench, an unfamiliar novel (turned to page one), dangling in her hands; to my right was a fat, white man, engrossed in an oily *roti*, and a disinterested East Indian lady to whom he was complaining that he was here only to secure tablets to curtail his cholesterol and blood pressure; an unlikely couple was sitting on the adjoining bench. Then there was the red-skinned fellow, still slouched against the open gate and casting wild sideway glances as if he'd had a premonition that he would be robbed.

Suddenly, the giant swung open the office door, and a funereal torpor engulfed the courtyard but Roxanne lurched from her seat and hurried across the courtyard, intercepted a woman at the entrance and disappeared inside. Seconds later, she returned with a dog-eared, yellow card, fit for the bin, and held it up for me to read. I said:

"Oh, he works by a number system?"

"Yes, he does!" Roxanne was legendary for her abrupt sentences and purism. "You see, Lyndon, a lot of people arrive early. He's an excellent doctor, you know, and quite cheap. It's only forty dollars per visit."

"That *rel* cheap," I confirmed in colloquial Trinidadian dialect. "It good to see it have *ah* doctor that still care about *poor* people."

The white man adjacent to us coughed, but Roxanne continued:

"He also does a lot of nice things for children. Every December he sponsors a party with lots of toys and…"

I interjected:

"Roxanne, you know, girl, I'm really worried about my testicles. I feel I'm going to lose them. Can you imagine what it would be like to have one balls?"

"It's one ball," she corrected, "and no, I can't imagine what it *will* be like."

With a chuckle of my own, I added:

"Especially in our family, girl. I mean, you could imagine the heckling that would take place?"

"Lyndon, don't blight yourself. You will be okay." She explained that inside the office she had secured position six but the unpleasant, red-skinned lady whom she had intercepted had protested, even though she herself had managed to lift card nine. However, Roxanne, being the good Christian that she was, had conceded to the lady's tantrum and allowed her to take her place, but they didn't exchange their cards. While I bewailed, she joked: "I got a six for a nine."

Time crept by.

One hour later, I was an impatient patient and unable to further bear the moans and groans of the sick so I stood and walked to the door, distributing more weight to my left foot. The reception area was a small, hermetic room filled with females sitting in chairs lined up along the walls as if it were a wake, and to the centre was a rickety coffee table, partially hidden by a dishevelled stack of outdated magazines that might have been there since the inauguration of the practice. A lopsided poster hung from the partition facing the entrance and dictated, in handwriting as crooked as a stick, that the office was twenty-five years old. To the left of the poster was the door which led to the doctor's office with a yellow number five (the current patient) drooped on it. When I stuck my head further inside, I noticed the secretary's desk nestled in a small rectangular area, filled with dozens of cream boxes holding patients' profiles, and barricaded with a crude burglar-proof gate because times had worsened.

I signalled to Roxanne and she closed her book on page one and scurried across just as Patient Five exited the doctor's private area. You might recall that my Christian cousin had, through verbal contract, allowed the red-skinned woman to proceed ahead of her without exchanging cards. I watched as Patient *Nine* hurried towards the door, slapped her card to the protruding nail and disappeared. It is only now as I write this, two days after I have been discharged from the Port of Spain General Hospital, that I can appreciate the comedy of the ordeal, however, at the time I was incensed and exclaimed:

"*Jeezanages*! The person with card ten going and think they next!"

I abandoned the thought and focussed on an archaic television which was fastened to the far corner of the wall that met the security gate. The stupidest programme I had ever seen was being aired, a game show where the winners were promised a spectacular trip to New Zealand; however, the genius twist to the apparent daily broadcast was: the contestants were homosexual couples. A girl of no more than six sat next to her mother, absorbed by the host and lesbian duos as they exchanged infantile questions and incongruous answers. Roxanne, guided by an impetuous force, declared:

"How absurd!"

I utilised the distraction to enquire whether or not

she believed that any of the other patients were here to lose their testicles.

"They're all female," she scolded and flipped her book open to page one.

In the process of time, Patient *Nine* exited with the same, red-skinned fellow who had been hunched over the gate. Immediately, an elderly East Indian lady stood, dusted the front of her shocking, blue sari, and hurried to the door while my cousin ambled towards her. I looked on from the outside as Roxanne, all business-like, stalled her and professed:

"Excuse me, ma'am. I'm sorry but we are next. I have the number six."

The *tanty* looked at Roxanne and the unbalanced number nine then matter-of-factly announced:

"I have number ten! The door have number nine so I am next!"

Without another word she hurried inside.

Not only did my heart crack but my pain also escalated and I silently hoped that the senior citizen did not have an end-of-the-year grocery list of maladies. To my surprise, however, Roxanne signalled for me to follow and with an impetus I tailed her and the old lady who was already unleashing a catalogue of lamentations. Inside the aseptic but sterile office, we tiptoed past the diseased woman and the seated doctor into a smaller, drearier room screened with an indeterminate pattern of white, floor-length cotton curtains and wooden walls. Inside, the antiseptic was thicker and there was a bed as narrow as a gurney wrapped in a seamless, white sheet (which I secretly hoped I wouldn't have to lie on), a frayed ottoman – which Roxanne occupied – a table decorated with flagons, and varnished shelves which housed oodles of ancient, medical apparatuses. Like a curious but cautious kid, I inspected the unfamiliar articles until my eyes landed on a shoebox filled with bloody cotton swabs. Immediately, my interest was deadened and I gingerly navigated to the bed adjacent to Roxanne, whose eyes were still glued to page one of her book. I said in a nervous whisper:

"Roxanne," and when she looked up I continued, "I'm really scared about losing my testicles."

I laughed; when I am nervous I laugh.

The doctor entered. His name was Shiva Narine and he had a face as ancient as his apparatuses, a sharp Roman nose which accented his stern eyes, and thinning but long hair. He didn't possess the kind, gentle aura of a pristine doctor, on a television advert, who had supposedly taken the Hippocratic Oath. Rather, Dr. Narine had wild, beady eyes which danced between Roxanne and me. He must have ascertained my nervousness because with a raspy voice he enquired of me:

"Whom am I seeing today?"

Dr. Narine's voice was a cauldron bubbling with the air of simplicity, experience and reassurance which I had been yearning for. Then, without warning, nostalgia swept over me and I was a child sitting on the hassock Roxanne now occupied, my tiny legs swinging to and fro, conscious of the concerned eyes and fidgeting hands of my mother, and aware of every cold jab of the dreaded chill ring of Dr. Narine's stethoscope. Roxanne cast a fleeting glance my way and the doctor's horn-rimmed glasses turned upon me, culminating the nausea that had temporarily subsided in my stomach. I hesitated because while it was tolerable to discuss my dilemma with my female cousin, it was awkward to do so in the presence of the doctor.

"Well?" he inquired.

I stuttered my poignant testimony and to my disappointment, for I had hoped to be cured by word of mouth, Dr. Narine instructed me to strip and lie down. Then he vanished behind the wooden partition. I stripped to my boxers, sniffed my armpits and somewhat satisfied by the resulting scent lay down. The bed was a trifle too short and, discomforted, I bent my feet and curled my toes against the wall. Behind the panel I heard the doctor enquiring about the old lady's family – *and tanty giving him the whole rundown about who married, dead and have more children and for whom.* I thought: is he mad? Did he not know that *my* testicles were aching? For the first time, I felt like no one was taking my problem seriously. The doctor reappeared abruptly and scolded my disobedience.

"Should I take off my boxers?" I asked honestly.

"How else do you expect me to see the problem?"

He disappeared again and behind the partition the long lamentation of Patient Ten resumed. I lunged from the bed as with the croaking of an old piece of furniture, and tugged the curtain shut until a disinterested Roxanne vanished from view. I removed my boxers, cupped my groin and lay down again, trusting that the bed sheet wasn't also celebrating its twenty-fifth anniversary and had been sanitised since its last usage.

Dr. Narine, the beloved workaholic, reappeared, equipped with surgical gloves and unknowingly he became the first of many who would inspect my testicles over the next few days. The sensation of the pungent, moist latex was not arousing, as I had dully and fearfully imagined it would have been, yet stupidly I concluded that this was due to the masculinity of the medical expert. I closed my eyes, but failed to gain comfort within the darkness of my mind and Dr. Narine must have sensed my distress because he said:

"Do you know that the last time you were here, you were two years old?"

A severe squeeze jolted my privates, as if he intended to learn why I hadn't visited more frequently, but before I could shriek a response, he pried:

"Does it hurt when I do this?"

I nodded; his index finger and thumb felt like a vise clamping my right testicle.

He probed around some more, squeezing my testicles here and there like a medicine ball, then suddenly stopped, removed his gloves, told me to clad myself quickly and without waiting for me to do so pulled the curtain back, revealing Roxanne. He assumed the tone of a calm businessman but his face betrayed a strenuous mark which worried me:

"This is serious. You have a condition known as testicular torsion but, thank goodness, it's only rudimentary. You need immediate surgery or you will lose your right testicle." When he perceived my confusion, he smoothly flipped to the argot of the grassroots: "It have lines that does carry blood to your balls. Sometimes they could twist with motion. It does not have to be a strain; it can be anything and when that happens it becomes *kinked* thereby preventing blood to keep the testicles alive. If they don't get blood for a long time your balls could die and you basically have to cut them off."

Dr. Narine looked at me; I looked at Roxanne; she looked at Dr. Narine. He paused, patted his pockets as if he had lost something and finally found the pad and pen he sought in his shirt jacket. He scribbled some hurried, illegible lines, tore the sheet from the pad and passed it to me.

"Take this to Mount Hope," he ordered, "and they will treat your situation as an emergency... you know you're the second case of torsion I've seen today!"

His revelation, though astounding and melodramatic, neither surprised me nor offered the quantum of solace which I sought; at least, however, I hadn't been the first naked man he had examined for the day. Without warning, my world smashed into the sun and ironically Roxanne and I had heard 'testicular *tersian*,' during Dr. Narine's extensive discussion. For the next few hours she and I would quote 'tersian' to persons monitoring me via cellular phones, a word which I thought sounded like all the males of Sparta had succumbed to groin injury.

I paid Dr. Narine forty dollars and filtered out of his office, past the patients in the reception area and back into the open environment where *life* was in full swing – strangely, the thought which bothered me the most was: why was the secretary behind a locked gate and it was the doctor who collected the fees? Things were as they had been earlier: gravel-laden dump trucks were still swerving madly through the intersection as if it were an empty stretch, inured taxi drivers were hustling prospective passengers, ribald dogs were sniffing each other's backside, cosmopolitan sots were soliciting – *'a lil small change, please'* – those scurrying to work, thick and thin crowds were huddled around doubles men – the crowd's thickness dependent on each vendor's reputation – and the sick were still filtering to the doctor. Things were as they had been, only busier, with a myriad of cars and people and a bigger, yellower sun, gleaming as in a touristy poster, but to the natives it was just another hot day and another cause for the remark, 'Gosh, boy, it hot like hell eh?' Agitated by the din of man and machine, I dialled my boss and relayed my heartrending dilemma which required immediate surgery.

"It's known as testicular tersian," I said confidently, spelling the ailment slowly, and suggesting that he *Google* it.

Any other memory I have of Dr. Narine's office is fragmentary for there are gaps I cannot explain and answers I have denied, for questions I cannot recount, but there are fears which are alive even to this day.

Roxanne was driving along the westbound highway on the outskirts of the neighbourhood where I lived and little did I know that I wouldn't be returning home for a few days and, if someone had prophesised this, I would have laughed despite my pain. As a transient Trincity slipped past, I wondered about my executive tempered glass desk and new bed.

After a series of mobile conversations and the speedy exchange of shaky ideas among female relatives, my fate was decided: I was to be taken to Mount Hope, the same hospital where my mother had intrepidly survived the labour pains I had administered a quarter of a century before. I was intimate with the place, having attended a college which strangely enough had been housed at the medical facility. Without warning, I began sobbing and vainly attempted to console myself by glancing between the blinking digital display on the van's dashboard and the fleeting outside world, hoping that time would freeze or my pernicious dream would end.

It was nine o'clock and I still had my two testicles.

Mount Hope Hospital

Mount Hope Hospital was an array of dusty, cube-shaped, cream buildings which looked like they had popped up from nowhere and contrasted sharply with the fertile landscape around the expanse of the compound. Where there wasn't concrete there was curvaceous, green grass and poui trees, and where there wasn't curvaceous, green grass and poui trees there was concrete.

Someone, perhaps a man, once said that the surest and fastest way to transfer news was via telephone, telegraph and tell-a-woman. Thus, by the time Roxanne's van manoeuvred into the compound my entire maternal family, from Trincity to Icacos, was already rolling the words 'testicular tersian' from quivering lips, all save my parents who had departed Trinidad two days before for a brief stint by my spectacular Aunt Barbara living in Toronto, Canada. I remained adamant that it was best not to ruin their trip which had been inspired by the bereavement of Uncle John – my dear aunt's husband, and a lover of literature and Trinidad's finest rum punch – merely because of my right testicle.

Roxanne's cellular phone, along with mine, was ringing incessantly and while I was thankful for the warm, familiar voices of my aunts and uncles, my pain coupled with the idea of possible loss of a testicle rendered me an abrupt ignoramus on these courtesy calls. My male cousins, however, disparaged my manhood in crucial tones and shared never-ending lists of potential nicknames, all of which crassly included the number 'one,' and while I wasn't the slightest amused, I managed a scoff on occasions, even though I knew that the intensions of the well-wishers were innocuous.

Roxanne finally found a parking space, paces away from Accident and Emergency (A & E) but my handicap made the distance wearisome. I hopped from the van and purposely moseyed ahead of Roxanne until I came to a curved ramp which led past an automatic door and into a reception area with a mass of people queued to see a male receptionist protected by a glass cage that extended to the ceiling. Overseeing the activity were two burly security personnel and I quickly surmised that A & E was rougher than Dr. Narine's office. I secretly hoped that I didn't have to join the line but Roxanne glided through the automated doors and said:

"We have to join this line."

She filtered in behind a man who smelled like a box of stillborn puppies that had been left in the sun for days, and who had a scabrous, diagonal gash which began at his forehead, ran over his left eyebrow and ended at his jowl, a mark which gave him a critical finish. However, I did not feel sorry for him as only his looks were at risk and not his manhood.

While we waited, another patient joined the line, a

tall African with an unforgettable gangster's face, whose complexion hovered somewhere between red and black, and who might have been either in his late twenties or early thirties. He had gashes across the face, arms and neck, more lethal in appearance than the single stroke adorning the patient ahead of us, wounds which looked as if they had been put there by a wild animal. While I didn't know his story, his depraved diction necessitated guesses which might be pretty accurate because he was hostile and arrogant to such an exaggerated extent, I began doubting that he felt any physical hurt. At one point, when he strayed from the needle-straight queue for the hundredth time, a security guard, obviously crabbed but simultaneously cowed by the patient's antics, politely requested that he give clearance to a wheelchair-bound, demented, old woman engaged in licking her shoulder. In response the spiv cursed and demonstrated such a magnificent display of machismo and ignorance that I feared for myself, and leaned against the wall so that my back would not be to him.

Time dragged by at a drowsy pace until finally, our turn arrived. About the same moment the redneck was complaining loudly about the hospital needing more than one receptionist in an area where he alleged people were dropping dead like flies; I agreed with him. I sat before an East Indian man who might have been queer, decked in funereal attire: black shirt, black pants, black tie and mascara. For some strange reason I wondered if his shoes were black also, how many persons he had checked in and how many of them had died. He said:

"Good day, Sir."

I was impressed as I had never imagined that public

sector employees addressed citizens with such dignity. Temporarily, my faith increased but without any additional pleasantries he requested my letter of referral and asked a series of questions regarding my personal details, social lifestyle, etcetera, and when the tedious procedure was through, he attached the handwritten form to Dr. Narine's letter and bade me depart with what I guessed was a standard goodbye.

The most noticeable feature of the waiting room was the stink, lingering scent of *death* although there were more than fifty *living* people huddled together in the tight box. I averted my eyes to the floor but, 'through the door, first right, first window on your right,' was still pretty easy to find. I shoved the paper through a slim recess to a gloved nurse and wondered how much germs could be on the paper, and as he read it, I reluctantly decided against mentioning that my problem was severe, despite Dr. Narine's advice; I couldn't, not with an army of incapacitated persons including the old woman – who was still licking her shoulder – waiting. I was told to sit. I began making my way to a rear seat but changed my mind when I saw the smelly guy two chairs away. Without warning, the loudspeaker cackled to life and three seats became free. While the other dejected patients sighed and resumed simmering in the gloominess of their burden, Roxanne and I quickly grabbed the seats and added the warmth of our backsides to the stiff plastic in preparation for what would turn out to be the longest wait of my life.

I can only describe the conditions of the hospital as deadly, and I say this not in ignorance, but having sat and absorbed the complicated arrangement which I shall now attempt to describe to you: the room was hermetic and dense with the stifling aroma of the diseased embalmed with ointments which brought no release, but rather the imaginary consolation that they would, in one way or another, lessen the agonies of the multitude. Taciturn patients, scattered throughout the room, had assumed eclectic, haphazard positions along the pews of hard metal chairs jointed to each other, while their companions stood or sat and sought to massage and whisper their ailments away. The milieu was a revolting merger of sickness and dishevelment, rendering it difficult and in some cases impossible to distinguish the sick from the well.

Two hours dragged by, a period in which my pain had doubled, insomuch that both acorns ached tremendously. I reread a bulleted notice painted onto a charcoal-board in white, cursive letters which stood out as a blatant contradiction to the wretched environment and stipulated in seven abrupt points that patients were not attended to according to their order of arrival but rather based on the severity of their problem. Therefore I assumed, based on Dr. Narine's fatal description, that I should have been atop this invisible list with every doctor and nurse in the hospital attending to me and sapping my head with the same soothing ointments which nauseated me.

However, I waited and waited.

For the second time I felt like no one was taking my problem seriously, but consoled myself by the selfless ideal that perhaps there were people in the very room who were suffering a great deal more than I was, and might have had their lives hanging from a brittle cord. Immediately behind me was an African girl who, though thin as a stick and tall as a lamppost, was literally curled into a tiny ball with her knees stuck to her breasts, and her hands wrapped around her ankles. She lay crying in the arms of a cockeyed guy who seemed to be staring in my direction each time I reacted to her unsettling moans. To the front, closer to window where patients submitted their forms, were two ancient but collective chaps who looked as though death had forgotten them, leaving them hunched over wheelchairs. I was genuinely glad when they were wheeled away after two unpronounceable names had been muffled over the public address system.

Sometime during that tiresome course of waiting, Roxanne disappeared and I was left alone in the room that was heavy with silence except for uncontrollable groans. For the first time the reality of sickness stuck its foot in a door that could not be closed, and stepped into my life. I had always thought of gatherings as fantastic events where males and females assembled regardless of age to pursue a common goal, for example: a football match, a strike, a congregation, a choir, or a party of sinners. However in the reception area, while the unique goal is seeing the doctor, there is no chance to explore team spirit or extend a comforting word; it is as if you exist alone despite the company of family or friends and solitude can only be found in small measures, if any at all, in the weakness of your mind as it unsuccessfully tries to shun pain.

It was around lunch time when Roxanne returned with Eva Borde, my girlfriend, who was dressed for work and whose paler-than-usual fingers were wrapped around a cylindrical stack of papers that I guessed were leaflets on *testicular tersian.* I shifted to the centre seat and grimaced more than smiled when they sandwiched me:

"Hi. How are you doing?"

"Lyndon! You don't know how serious this thing is! You can lose that testicle if you aren't careful and do you know what that means?" she murmured in a fine, continuous breath as was her usual parlance.

I shrugged.

"Lyndon, that means you are producing half the amount of sperm and if you can't produce sperm then the chances of you having–" she looked around suspiciously then continued in a lowered voice– "the chances of us having children are slim. What if you lose the next ball?"

"Who the heck is thinking about kids?" I frowned. "Goodness! My baby-makers are dying and you're talking about kids?"

It suddenly dawned on me that the scrotums did indeed have something to do with procreation. *I am doomed*, I thought, aghast that the potential of losing my left testicle had been brought into the equation, and the nervousness of my friend, who was obviously anxious to suckle young ones, bewildered me. I felt that while her mental turmoil was warranted, her pronouncement that my *other* ball was threatened had been grossly insensitive. My mind retracted into a dark hole and beyond seeing blurs, I can recount no exact detail except that I nodded or shook my head at the familiar but imperceptible voices around me.

I requested the time at the point when I had exhausted all the quasi-comfortable positions. It was three o'clock and I was suddenly aware of how angry and hungry I was.

My name still hadn't been announced and I was weary of waiting and staring at the speaker with insatiable hope that the next patient ordered inside would have been Lyndon Baptiste. After a string of mobile conversations and angry outbursts, I halfheartedly decided to exit the dreary waiting room.

Roxanne and I walked reluctantly to her vehicle while Eva went ahead to park her car at home; we would travel in a single vehicle. With each limp, I fantasised that the next name called in the waiting room was mine and I was uncertain whether or not I had made the right decision to leave. As we exited the compound, I buried the idea and once a more homely dressed Eva had been picked up, we began the journey to Port of Spain via a highway eased of traffic.

As we neared the capital, I requested the handouts which Eva still clutched. The first bore Wikipedia's logo and the headline shouted: *Testicular Torsion*. It had previously occurred to me that *tersian* was a peculiar word and I purposed to correct my vocabulary for the benefit of imminent doctors and well-wishers, and myself. I skimmed through the first few paragraphs pulling the snippets which mattered most *viz.*:

"In testicular torsion the spermatic cord that provides the blood supply to a testicle is twisted, cutting off the blood supply, often causing orchalgia. Prolonged testicular torsion will result in the death of the testicle and surrounding tissues. In most males, the testicles are attached to the inner lining of the scrotum. Males whose attachment is higher up are at risk of testicular torsion. This condition is known as a bell clapper deformity (as in the central piece of a bell) and

is a major cause of testicular torsion. A male who notices the ability of either or both testicles to freely rotate within the scrotum should be aware that he is at risk of testicular torsion. Testicles that are in a much lower position and/or in a slightly rotated position in the scrotal sack are a visual indicator of this risk. Torsions are sometimes called "winter syndrome." This is because they often happen in winter, when it is cold outside. The scrotum of a man who has been lying in a warm bed is relaxed. When he arises, his scrotum is exposed to the colder room air. If the spermatic cord is twisted while the scrotum is loose, the sudden contraction that results from the abrupt temperature change can trap the testicle in that position. The result is a testicular torsion. With prompt diagnosis and treatment the testicle can be saved in a high number of cases. Testicular torsion is a medical emergency that needs immediate treatment. After 6 hours there is about 12% chance of saving the testicle, and after 8 hours the possibility is decreased further. Once the testicle is dead it must be removed to prevent gangrenous infection. A simple and minor surgery will correct and prevent testicular torsion. It can be done in an emergency situation after determination that the testicle is cut off from blood supply or as an outpatient procedure for patients who have experienced frequent episodes with testicular torsion. If necessary, the surgeon will first untwist the testicle(s). The surgeon will then permanently suture the testicles to the inner lining of the scrotum. If only one testicle has been problematic, the surgeon may suture both testicles as a preventative effort."

After perusing the articles, I flung the papers onto the backseat and although it felt as if I had been reading for over an hour, when I looked up we were still a great distance from the city. I was frustrated and hammered my mind as to the cause of my problem. There were a few factors, none that I could have ruled out, yet none that I could have fingered definitely. Firstly, there was the gym, however, I didn't lift very heavy weights and a related problem might have been hernia; then there was the fact that I had recently installed an air-conditioner, but I rarely used it and the temperature was incapable of being as cold as *in winter*; lastly, there remained the probability that I had longer-than-normal testicles which allowed my bells to clap more freely. I scoffed.

Meanwhile, Roxanne made a timely judgment and bypassed the Beetham, choosing instead a route which took us over a winding, mountainous road that placed us on the outskirts of the heart of the capital. We exited the base of the Lady Young and turned onto another lazy highway which took us along the Queen's Park Savannah, fetching every red traffic light along the way. At an intersection, a car pulled alongside, the notes of a popular Latin song wafting through its windows. The few phrases I managed to grasp from the love ballad were, 'you're still the *one* I need the most,' 'walk *freely* with me,' 'stand by my *side* forever' and 'we will always be *together*.' I managed a laugh. Maybe the songwriter had received a premonition about my testicular pain and had made a hit song to commemorate my dilemma. Roxanne and Eva asked what was so hilarious.

"That song," I said, pointing to the car.

The traffic light blinked to green and the car sped off, and while we followed, I explained the connection between the melody and my gonads. A light moment ensued and we spent the duration of the drive conjuring up song titles which matched my situation, oblivious to the spectacular view of the capital on an otherwise beautiful day. Some titles included 'With or without you,' 'One more time,' altered into, 'One more ball,' and, 'You're still the one I need the most,' by an artist I am still unfamiliar with. Then, without warning, I plummeted into a sombre mood but the traffic flowed freely and in little time we arrived at *Special Care Associates of Medicine.*

The time was three-thirty and I still had my two testicles.

Special Care Associates of Medicine.

◇◇◇◇◇◇◇◇◇◇◇◇◇◇◇◇◇◇◇◇◇◇◇◇◇

S.C.A.M. was a plush building of the Victorian epoch nestled on the corner of a busy crossroad. The facility's spacious car park was equipped with some of the most luxurious vehicles I had ever seen in Trinidad and Tobago, and while this fact relayed a lucid message to me, I concluded that money was the least pressing of my concerns as I was in unbearable pain and hardly able to stand. All I yearned for was someone, anyone, to inspect my ball and confirm that it was alive and swinging, although I had secretly resigned myself that my right testicle was lost, reasoning based on the chasm in medical attention. In good humour, I had even envisioned a twenty-one gun salute funeral, complete with a tiny flag draped over the deceased, entombed in a used matchbox. I wobbled along, choosing the ramp rather than the concrete staircase and once past the security booth, the automatic doors closed behind Roxanne, Eva and I.

We had entered another world; the air was fragranced

to a sickening proportion, and lush purple carpeted the elaborate reception area, void of patients. Busied administrative staff attired in stiff, starched clothes and powdered, frowning faces smiled upon eye contact, an automated rather than natural process which betrayed something I couldn't quite figure. Hosts of support staff appeared, as if by magic, armed with immaculate wheelchairs after being paged by a saintly, honey-voiced announcement over the flawless address system. The place truly was enchanted, I thought, but as I would learn, most tricks came at a high cost to the audience.

I stood while Roxanne went to the front desk where three ladies had their heads buried in computer screens and never-ending sheets of papyrus. Before Roxanne could mutter a word, a tall, smiling, dark-skinned lady slid into view, a woman who looked like she had spent the previous night greasing her hair to her skull. One hand manacled the other and her huge smile portrayed, *I don't really smile this big but you've got to have money to be here so I will do it for you.* This same lady politely, no furtively, highlighted that she was at Roxanne's whim and fancy.

From where I stood, Roxanne's words were inaudible but the confused look on her communicator's face clarified that she had never heard of "testicular torsion" and my cousin's repetition, slower each time, did nothing to enlighten her. When she finally assembled the pieces, she repeated it loudly, causing the other female staff to look towards where I stood, a few feet away. The woman asked:

"Who has testicular torsion?" She pointed at me, the only male in the room: "Him?"

Eva was beside me and nothing about her languid features suggested that she was a victim of an ailment exclusive to boys and men. At that moment, a muscular man in his twenties, the same one who had won employee of the quarter according to a gilded, framed picture where he sported jerry curls, entered the reception area. He stopped, looked at each one of us, and with an expression of recognition pointed at Eva:

"Someone called this morning asking about testicular torsion. Was it you?"

I guessed that either the voice had sounded Caucasian to him or he was punctilious.

Eva nodded; she explained that apart from browsing the World Wide Web she had made some calls.

Kevin, as his nametag read, continued in a high-pitched voice which was inconsonant with his physique:

"Yes! I did not know what it was but I telephoned around. I did not have your number so I apologise if you thought that I had forgotten." Then to highlight his new-found knowledge he spoke pedantically for a lengthy time about testicular torsion, pronouncing testicle in such a manner that it sounded more like 'spectacle'; during his speech the lady who had first approached Roxanne stood smiling, looking rather revealed that *S.C.A.M.* was in fact familiar with the disorder. It was obvious why Kevin had won employee of the quarter and I assumed that based on his extensive knowledge he would easily secure the award a consecutive time. Finally, he wrapped up his mini lecture and confirmed that a specialist had been contacted and was en-route to the private hospital.

"Yes! We know all about testicular torsion," the female

worker added, "and the specialist will be here shortly. In fact he deals with it all the time!"

I was impressed for I had been inside for less than five minutes, and had only known the employee of the quarter for under two; yet, a consultant was already on his way. Their task completed, Kevin and the oily-head clerk disappeared behind the reception area with the promise of arranging any facility I desired.

Twenty minutes later, I was still standing because of the pain generated from sitting. Eva and Roxanne appeared rather comfortable seated on lavish lounge chairs. Pompous patients were being pushed to and from the entrance in wheelchairs, and I couldn't help but notice the stark contrast in the appearance of the workers and the sick. The labourers were almost always male and looked void of job excitement and weary of the sick. The manner of the patients however was dependent on whether they were being wheeled into or leaving the administration. Those entering didn't appear that ill to me. In fact, they looked like they could have gotten the same results from a general practitioner or a cheap pack of painkillers; however, those being swept out rode with largo and did nothing to hide their conceit.

Twenty-five minutes later, Ms. Oily-head stuck her face outside. Shocked, she asked:

"What are you all still doing here?"

"Shouldn't I be asking you that?" I shrugged.

She hurried through the door separating the reception area from the administrative staff and transformed into a pathetic creature, showering me with apologies and beseeching me to sit so that I wouldn't bring more bodily harm to myself. She grieved:

"I was under the impression that support staff had wheeled you to the Emergency Section."

I was furious but concealed it magnificently with a fallacious smile.

She disappeared and after another sweet-lipped command for, "a support staff member and wheelchair in the reception area, a support staff to the reception area please," an East Indian man, clothed in surgeon's garb, appeared immediately as if he had been anxiously waiting just out of sight beyond the long, narrow hall.

I sat and with the same torpor was wheeled through a labyrinth of iridescent corridors. *S.C.A.M.* was bigger than it had looked from the outside, I figured, but finally we halted at a counter where at least a dozen doctors and nurses were standing idly. I clambered out of the wheelchair and noticed with some surprise that everyone was smiling at me. I had heard fairytales of the animosity of medical professionals but apparently the instigators of such fables had never visited *Special Care Associates of Medicine*. I thought that the service was spectacular for around me was a company of faultless professionals clad in spotless white coats, personnel whose faces added to my sentiment a mysterious mix of adoration, happiness, pity, kindness and forgiveness. It appeared also like a crucible, filled with love, pity, sadness, reverence, fear and loathing, and laced with hot malice so crimson it could neither be understood nor explained. Immediately, I forgave the initial *balls-up*. A thick, African nurse, dressed in baby blue with black trimmings, and who shone like she had been polished, bellied up to me. Her teeth were as white as snow and her hair long and shimmering, and covertly I wondered whether or not slick hairdos were a criterion for employment at the private facility.

"What seems to be your problem?" she asked in a bright, bubbly voice as if I were an old friend she had stumbled upon years later.

I decided that I liked her disposition and responded frankly:

"I have a balls problem."

Surprised at my bluntness, the nurse bent upon me a glance of astonishment and waited for the truth, but I repeated myself, clearer and louder each time. She blinked rapidly as if processing a response and, still speechless and shaking her head incredulously, reached over to a nearby table and slipped on a pair of gloves. She motioned for me to follow her into a wider room which contained an array of empty beds but if there were other patients, they were hidden by royal blue curtains adorned with an overkill of yellow stars and yawning grey moons. The nameless nurse indicated a bed, chucked into a corner as if an afterthought, and I obediently lay, facing a white wall which needed another coat of paint; strangely I didn't think of my quasi-painted bedroom at home. Stencilled on the wall was the number six. For the second time in one day I had been assigned the same digit and for the second time in one day I was on a stretcher that was too small for me. What a sick coincidence, I gibed, paying more attention to my misfortunes than the *comfort* of knowing that nearby were medical professionals.

Having no pillow, I interlocked my fingers behind my nape and scanned the room. To my right, were beds and around each were squares made of metal, fastened to the ceiling and burdened with the gaudy, floor-length curtains. Each section was a clone of the other, containing the same assortment of futuristic but unfamiliar medical gizmos. Area Six was exactly the same except smaller. Roxanne and Eva reappeared and moved to sit on wicker chairs contiguous to my bed. Before they could settle, a hairy-as-a-gorilla doctor who smelled like a walking ashtray, invaded and introduced himself by a name I cannot recall. He ordered me to undress then disappeared. Roxanne asked:

"Do you want me to stay?"

I shook my head.

"Would you like me to?" Eva asked hopefully.

"No thanks," I replied and they left, Eva looking as if I had broken her heart.

When Doctor Gorilla returned, he was wearing latex gloves and I was standing naked, my legs opened like a voracious scissors and my hands clasped behind my back. He bent over and I was immediately saturated with the hot fear that I would earn an erection while he *fondled* me in search for some unknown *thing*. After each squeeze, twist and turn he looked up, and with a smirk asked how I felt. I sincerely believe that he was gay and this assumption is not based on the notion that my testicles drooped in his hands for an extended length… of time. To hasten the process, I groaned agonisingly at each touch, and at one point, the confused chap brought his gloved hand to his bottom lip and stroked it in bothered contemplation. Then, realising his flagrant error, he disappeared. Minutes later, Roxanne and Eva reappeared along with an administrative staff member who thrust a pad and pen in my face.

"What's that?" I asked. "A death disclaimer?"

She wasn't amused, but Roxanne quickly rescued the scene, explaining that it was a contract wherein I was committing myself to an initial five-hundred-dollar deposit and the payment of all medical expenses incurred during my stay. After a set of byzantine formalities, I scrawled my name adjacent to the *x* and the manikin disappeared.

A few seconds later, the bubbly nurse reappeared and after much coaxing, I learnt her name: Nurse Claire. To me, the prefix *Nurse* was absolutely peculiar. After taking my pressure she disappeared. Instantaneously, another nurse equipped with vials and needles materialised and explained that she needed a blood sample. I have a perpetual fear of needles and was amazed at the crudeness of the science and the length and breadth of the ones she possessed. I closed my eyes and focussed on an eccentric, deceased doctor – a man whom I recall each time I whiff camphor and whose office I dreaded as a child, the first practitioner to administer my first *mosquito bite* – while the nurse executed her job with deft precision. She slithered away with a quiet goodbye. Immediately, another nurse confronted me; I needed an antibiotic shot in my hip. I wondered: was there a different nurse for every job in this place? I careened and with the antibiotic shot came the severe cramping of my thigh and backside, a cramp which I felt certain was the exact one which drowned swimmers. My back arched and locked against my legs, forming a C, and I remained there, thoroughly engrossed by my discomfort, but distracted from my testicles for the first time in hours – but that night I would still be in pain, suffering random spasms and cramps in my lower back. When the *Injection*

Nurse disappeared, the *Document Nurse* reappeared with a contract dictating that I was allowing Dr. Maharaj to see me. I signed hastily and she left.

The curtains bucked back with a metallic grating, and Dr. Maharaj announced himself with the irruption of a magician. He was a tall, mixed man with an affable face and an aura which leaked intelligence. His look was completed by square, gilted spectacles that sat on a Roman nose, and muddled hair that slashed his age to that of a schoolboy although light streaks of grey decorated his crown. He offered a hand and needlessly introduced himself. Then straight to business:

"Drop them."

I felt like a villain with a gun, and maybe I was. I dropped my pants, erecting Dr. Maharaj to position three, and without request he began massaging my testicles with bare hands. He noticed my surprise and returned a smile, reconfirming that he was *The King of Balls*, but from where I lay I tasted my sweat and my embarrassment did not recede like an ebbing tide. Seeking escape, I closed my eyes, as I had done in Dr. Narine's office, and answered an onslaught of questions:

"Do I have diabetes? No, no diabetes. No hypertension, false teeth, sexual intercourse, family with diabetes, family with hypertension, family with false teeth, family who had sexual intercourse… or family with similar problems." When I was uncertain, I simply said no.

In lecturer's fashion, he defined testicular torsion and after a period of long, slow silence, he confirmed, with a bobbing head, that I would need a *fixation* surgery.

"I want to ensure, however, that you have not

succumbed to a potential infection," he warned with his infallible smile, "so we need to check that the testicle is still alive. You need an ultrasound."

Then he left to concoct a referral letter addressed to a facility located in the heart of Port of Spain. As fast as he disappeared, I was out of bed and dressed. I divided the curtains only to see a thoughtful Dr. Maharaj standing, giving directions to Roxanne while he scribbled on a pad that he held at eyelevel. When she asked whether or not Charlotte Street ran up or down, he scratched his face which wore a mask of uncertainty.

Certainly he did not have time to wash his hands, I thought.

Even as we made our way to the car park, I was still laughing to myself: so far three people had seen me naked.

It was near four-thirty and I still had my two testicles.

The coolness of transmission gel

Even though we had a mini map to the radiologist's office, we wasted time taking wrong turns as the streets and landmarks on the drawing were labelled, to our confusion, in crisscrossed text which didn't correspond to the cardinality of the streets. I shuddered with each inexperienced circle as my ball's life hung in the noose, but finally Roxanne found the quaint, wooden building on the perimeter of a popular park. The cozy but cold office contained three of the most unpleasant people I had ever seen. I thought: most likely they are disgruntled. After transferring a down payment, I sat with Roxanne and Eva and discussed my confusion:

"Aren't ultrasounds designed for pregnant women only?"

They laughed and highlighted the functions of the device, one of which included a gizmo that had to be inserted into the female's reproductive passage.

"Thank goodness my testicles aren't in my buttocks," I gaffed.

Suddenly, a riled Pakistani accent filtered into the wintry reception area:

"I am truly blest! Do I know if I am truly blest? Yes I know I am truly blest! I have money beyond my wildest dreams and tons of female customers."

The voice contained enough sarcasm to burst a dam but the conversation slued with the words, 'I love you,' followed by the loud slam of a telephone receiver. I hoped the peeved voice didn't belong to the person who would be attending to me, I whispered to Eva. Shortly after, a lady exited one of the many blue doors in the office and signalled to me. I followed her and once behind one of those very entrances, I found myself in a smaller, cozier, carpeted room equipped with a blanketed bed and a computer, the likes of which I had never seen before. A cylindrical device, the size of a small baton, was holstered in a cream plastic sack atop the control panel, and I humorously hoped that it wasn't an anal ultrasound machine. I was directed to a spot which hid the monitor's screen so to this day I am still at a loss as to what inside my testicles look like. The attendant indicated that I should remove my clothing and it dawned on me that she would be the first woman, since the starter gun of the experience had been fired, who would see me naked. Once on my back, she disappeared but returned with instructions to undress and cover myself with the green blanket beside the bed, as if she had forgotten this procedure.

"The *ultrasound man* is on his way," she rasped.

I lay half-naked, staring at the ceiling until a petit man, with the lean profile of a starved rat, entered and wordlessly began fiddling with the computer. He lifted the baton from its holding place and swung it in a pernicious manner. My buttocks were clenched tightly when he spoke:

"Drop the cloth please."

It was the same thick, Pakistani voice that I had heard. I did as instructed; there were now four notches on my gun. While I waited for further instructions, I prayed that I wouldn't be asked to rotate on my stomach; however no such indication was given. Instead, I felt non-greasy, ultra cold, ultrasound transmission gel being applied to my testicles. Then the baton was applied lightly. The gel became colder and under different circumstances it would have felt pleasant; however I was naked and still cautious that the gel might be lubricant in the event that a view from a different vantage was required.

Throughout the entire procedure, the *truly blest ultrasound man* was wordless and shifted his furtive glances, over the rim of his glasses, between the screen, a track pad on the panel and the rod on my staff. After fifteen minutes of wheeling and knob pressing, he ordered me to remove the gel then disappeared, but I opted to leave the substance since it brought a peculiar relief to my groin.

Outside, I collected the documents stapled securely in a tiny envelope, paid the balance and we left the cold reception room. I had just spent six hundred and thirty dollars on my testicles for a process that had taken under five minutes.

It was only then I realised that the health industry was a very lucrative business.

One night in heaven

◇◇

Back at *S.C.A.M.*, I collapsed into bed number six and waited with bent legs. My pain had somewhat subsided along with the frosty intensity of the transmission gel, but my skin was clammy. I was checking my armpits for foul scents when Dr. Maharaj reappeared and commanded me to 'drop them.' Wordlessly, I obeyed and again, with naked hands, he inspected my testicles. Later, I would learn that each time this man felt my seeds I paid him close to three hundred dollars and, oddly, it was only then that I felt satisfied that he had been barehanded; it made the inspection worthwhile. He adjusted his glasses and confirmed:

"Yes… we are going to have to commit you." He looked at me through jaundiced eyes as if expecting resistance and acquiring none concluded, "The injection you received earlier was an antibiotic so you will rest overnight and tomorrow we will take it from there."

In laconic fashion, I signalled okay and my liberator departed for the night. Once he was gone, Lisa appeared at my bedside. A languid hand was covering her mouth as she spoke:

"Lyndon, boy, how you going?"

My eldest sister is a cool cat yet stoic, hard as steel, straight as an arrow's shaft, sharp as its point and exactly balanced with a fletching, yet her concerned high-pitched voice and fluttering mannerisms at that moment might have deceived some to believe otherwise. I mentioned that my pain had somewhat decreased and that I was being kept for the night. A few more trivialities were exchanged then she got to the economics of the ordeal:

"Okay… it's something like seven hundred a night but how it works is that I have to make a seven-thousand-dollar deposit." She looked at me sideways. "Do you have that kind of money?"

I shook a suddenly heavier, dismal head.

"Well, that is okay. I will pay it using my credit card. It's unlikely, however, that you will use that amount anyway. How it works is that each day they deduct whatever money was spent on your account."

After five minutes I was lost by Lisa's financial wizardry. I felt like a louse and believed that she shouldn't be standing any expense on my behalf, especially with a scheduled family vacation just around the corner. Suddenly a dreary burden descended upon me. Finance, however, was a job which Lisa was born to do and even though I imagined my guilt to be perpetual, I knew that she would settle any score which arose. I believe it was my mother who once said that Lisa had been born with the Midas touch. However, I said nothing and shook my head through the detailed breakdown of monies: how it would be acquired, spent, distributed, collected, reimbursed and so forth. When she was through, she left with the promise of paying *S.C.A.M.* and acquiring toiletries for my use.

Once she was gone, Eva reappeared with a new visitor, her mother. Mrs. Borde was a stout woman with a touch of Portuguese aristocracy and long, tedious features which divulged neither interest nor disinterest. Like those before her, she enquired of my health and like other times I softened, through disguised smiles, the harshness of my pain. I answered her questions even though my mind drifted across some dismal plain; I had never slept in a hospital before.

Sometime later, a request for a support staff resonated over the sound system and it must have regarded me because an unfamiliar figure clad in brown appeared and stood attentively at my bedside. Nurse Claire returned and requested that I don my jeans. I declined. Haughtily, her mask dropped and she exclaimed impudently:

"But what is this? You want me to go all the way down to the laundry to get you a skirt?"

I longed to retaliate with the reminder of who paid her bills but decided against it, having heard stories and seen movies where nurses practised euthanasia and murder. Instead, I swathed using the long sheet which adorned the stretcher. I was formally wheeled out of the room, passing transient, medical eyes which focussed more on my testicles than on my face. Only one of the placid faces formed a soft smile and I cynically wondered how many of the employees would recount my sorry tale at home or over drinks.

The journey to the ward was a nightmare. The support staff that ushered me, along with Nurse Claire, apparently had no driving experience, or he either hated his job or disliked me for not complying and wearing my jeans. I was banged and rammed into every last wall as the stretcher shuddered through Gaza-thin corridors. Finally we came to a double door where Eva and her mother were told to wait. I heard the doors swing shut behind my head and after two more bangs I was admitted into Ward Seven.

It was after six o'clock and I still had my two testicles.

Ward Seven was a homely domain, a tad bigger than my bedroom and painted in a yellow similar to the one I had selected. It had matching curtains, the lower half of which was plaid and adorned with great red melons that would have best suited a kitchen, and any view of the outside world was hidden by a high wall which appeared quite ghastly in the approaching darkness. Ward Seven had been designed for rich comfort and included an awkwardly positioned television, jammed into one corner, with an air-conditioner unit beside it. To the west was a humongous chair which easily could have seated two obese adults, and an unplugged fan, its power cord wrapped around the rotating shaft. The room was trimmed by a white, smartly carved cornice, and the wall was sliced into two by a thick band of wallpaper which ran smartly around the full length of the ward. Robbing all this, however, was an intriguing bed which I thought might have belonged to the realm of sexual perversion. There were vertical pieces of iron at each corner post, burdening horizontal pieces that ran to either end, like scaffolding. I joked that it had been customised for a rich patient who worked in construction. Nurse Claire's voice abolished the serenity as she welcomed me to Ward Seven as if it were a suite:

"This is your room! It comes complete with a window, television and a bathroom which you will be sharing with the next door patient." She paused and pointed in the obvious direction. "So remember to knock! And this here is your bed… I hate this bed," she confessed bitterly, clenching its frame and frowning as if recalling some forlorn memory she had suppressed. "It's an orthopaedic bed."

"What's orthopaedic?" I asked. I was propped up on my elbows, still lying on the stretcher.

"Oh you know it's for people who have this, that, the other, broken bones and muscle deformities. They can just fling their slings over these handle bars." She grabbed a long, shiny chain which was coiled on the bed and animatedly threw it over the bars. "This chain can be used if you wish an attendant. You can just pull it like this."

She tugged on it and a few seconds later a nurse shoved open the double door. Nurse Claire dismissed her with a hostile wave, and indicated that I switch from the stretcher to the mattress. I obeyed, uncertain that my question had been answered as I had expected a demonstration of the bed's usage.

I'm tall, six feet four inches, and despite this, the bed was still pretty high for me. It was raised so far above the floor that I could see beneath it, and to the very centre there was a small, wooden, rectangular box with a white cross carved on top, an item which would persistently perturb and haunt me for the duration of my stay at the institution. I am not swayed by superstition but I would spend minutes at a time with my eyes glued to the inanimate object as if I expected some devilish phenomena to occur. I wondered: what was it for? It certainly wasn't a footstool for the royalty in the story: *The Princess and the pea*. Was it some relic which cleansed the room in the event of death? I promised myself to keep an eye on it.

Once I was in bed, the horrid driver left. Nurse Claire turned on the cooling system and attempted to demonstrate how to activate the television, but to my delight never succeeded. She suddenly looked weary and before leaving confessed:

"I hope your family was not upset that I asked them to wait outside. Your sister looked pretty angry when I did."

"That's okay," I said and meant it, "you have a job to do and I respect that." I omitted that Eva was not my sister.

When Nurse Claire left, I wondered whether her behaviour was genuine or specious due to the elitism *S.C.A.M.* practised. Some time elapsed before Eva and her mother appeared, Mrs. Borde looking careworn and collapsing in the chair. Surprised at its size, she asked whether or not it belonged to Gulliver. Eva, on the other hand, began inspecting every nook and cranny of the room and in her usual captious manner began offering her consternation at various features such as the morbid view and bizarre bed. This continued until Lisa returned with a bag filled with jockeys, jerseys, soap, toothpaste, a toothbrush, a towel and five grey rags. I wondered why there were so many rags but asked nothing of it. Lisa left with promises to see me the following day. I wanted to be alone, but Roxanne still had to return with food for Eva and me.

An endless hour later, Roxanne entered with a ton of aromatic food: fried chicken, jerked pork from St. James and fries. I placed my testicles on the back burner and after hard, long, never-ending goodbyes had been whimpered, I planned my night's itinerary: I would shower then do justice to these meals since I was hungry enough to eat a hippopotamus, and didn't have to be concerned about an operation anytime soon, but I would leave a bit of the jerk pork for a later hour, I reckoned, since it was my habit to consume food at ungodly hours. With my plan in place, I hit the showers, forgetting to bolt the door that led to the adjacent room.

Fifteen minutes later, I exited the cramped shower and with the skip of a heartbeat was startled to find a feeble, old man stooped over a contraption that appeared to be the fusion of a walker and a toilet. His buttocks were pressed against the wall, his hands clutched the sink in agony, his eyes were closed and the strain on his face shouted *constipation!* Maybe he was deaf because the water in the shower had been running hard for a long spell, but for his sake I was glad that I had forgotten to lock the door. I disappeared behind the shower curtains before he saw me and tolerated his groans and flatulence until he left. Hurriedly, I exited the shower and fidgeted with the door knob, careful not to touch the sink or the funny looking toilet he had been stooped over, until the door snapped shut. Obviously the wards linked to the bathroom were designed for the disabled, I reasoned, since the commode was abnormal; what I never figured from the toilet's special design was its proper use, since it had the appearance of a machine that accommodated triceps dips while bowels were released. I dressed, still trying to determine the function of the contraption, and exited the bathroom into the coolness of my *suite.*

As I got into bed an East Indian nurse entered the room after knocking but not waiting for a response. She was petite with hair that hadn't been combed for ages and cocked eyes that danced crazily behind her spectacles. I don't know if it was because of my fresh look or company policy but she was smiling from ear-to-ear. At my bedside, she enquired:

"Hi. How are you?" Her voice was slow and deliberate and her accent as thick as the *Ultrasound Man's*, but not Pakistani.

"I am fine and you?" I flirted.

She ignored me perhaps because she didn't understand my dialect or chose to, however she still smiled like a happy bride. She produced a pen and pad from behind her back as if they had been hidden by her garment's lapels and asked:

"Any valuables on you? Like cellular phone, jewels or a watch?"

I related that I had only a mobile phone. I asked for her name again. With a smile she gauged me thoughtfully then asked a list of questions similar to the ones I had completed on entry. I answered all as before and again asked her name. After a few more tries, she finally understood.

"Priya," she said shyly.

I wondered if Priya understood English and yearned to see what she had written on the pad.

"And where are you from, Priya?"

"India is my motherland," she boasted and after a few more questions and answers left.

I believe that eating is best enjoyed when one's favourite dish is consumed last. Therefore the fried chicken went first then the jerked pork, but a huge portion was left back for later. The banquet was consumed in minutes and I lay in bed switching positions constantly to ease digestion and pamper my testicles.

During this time, a nurse whom I had known since childhood and who was also employed by the medical firm visited and we began chatting lightly on everything except the reason I was at the private institution. I thoroughly enjoyed her company insomuch that I offered her some of the jerked pork.

"What! You have pork?" she exclaimed, making a euphonic sound, like a neighbour smelling a baking ham.

"Yeah, right here," I said, directing the bagged box towards her.

She received it graciously but rather than open it and extract a few pieces, she clasped the food and pressed it affectionately against her stomach, as if it were a child. Suddenly starved for conversation and fearing that I wouldn't retrieve my late night snack, I stuttered:

"So umm…" my insatiable eyes on the box, "what time are you working until?"

I think she was famished too, for pork that is, because she seemed suddenly anxious to leave. Patting the box, she grieved:

"Seven o'clock in the morning. Anyway, boy, I have to go. I have rounds to make."

I knew that what she didn't say was that she had

pork to devour. With a quick goodnight and a promise to visit again she exited, heading in a direction I didn't decipher, but guessed was the cafeteria; I would never see her again.

I lay brooding over the loss of the jerked pork and watching the black screen of the inactive television which reflected only Gulliver's chair. I had heard my father say on countless occasions that when one is sick, they lose all interest in flicks. I have an almost fatal attraction to television and that night there was not the slightest desire to have it switched on to hear its noise or relish the thrills which it is capable of displaying. Whereas some women enjoy soap operas because the characters' circumstances, even though real, are much more spiteful than theirs, a terminally or chronically ill person cannot tolerate problems which supplement sickness. I stared at the television for a long time until finally I wondered how to shut the lights off. I was about to pull the alert chain but noticed a cord, with a switch at one end, wrapped around a post on the orthopaedic bed. With some effort, I pulled myself up, switched off the lights and was immersed in the strange comfort of total darkness. Before closing my eyes, I checked that the box bearing the crucifix wasn't glowing ominously and hadn't shifted position and after I was absolutely certain I lay down. Minutes later I checked again. Nothing had changed. Nothing had changed, I convinced myself, and dozed off.

I awoke when the double door creaked open. The lights flickered angrily. It was Priya, bearing a handful of bandages, and a much older nurse who had a macula like a lightning bolt that extended over her left eye and disappeared beyond her hairline. I had never seen her before. I sat up and without a word the unfamiliar, taciturn face nudged along between the bed and the wall, and Priya stood where she had been earlier. I had a strange feeling that these nurses would be the first women to see me naked and I waited, hoping not, with my fingers crossed. They stood there in awkward silence, as if uncertain how to get me undressed. Then, without forewarning, the old lady almost commanded me to drop my pants.

I sincerely believe that if the gap between Priya's and the older nurse's age was narrower I wouldn't have felt hopeless, like a prisoner probably does when jail breaking and a spotlight suddenly pinpoints him. Priya looked too young to see a penis and perhaps the older woman hadn't glimpsed one in *donkey years*. I brooded: did they really need two nurses to do this job? Maybe the senior nurse had volunteered, I concluded wickedly.

With closed eyes I dropped my pants, but because my curiosity mounted I winked them open. Priya wore gloves and a wide smirk, and was clumsily running a hammock-shaped bandage around my testicles; when she was finished, she scotch taped either end to my stomach. Then she patted my left leg, an instruction for me to raise it, and ran another length of hair-tugging tape back around the scrotum and my right leg. During the entire operation, Nurse Ancient had my seeds cushioned with her bare hands, like one would when forming a cup with both hands. When they were through, my balls looked like they had been secured in a catapult, ready to be fired, and with satisfied smiles the nurses left me... humiliated.

I flicked off the light and went to sleep.

According to my cellular phone, I awoke at five o'clock the next morning with a searing pain that felt like my right testicle was being ripped off every few seconds, thrown to the ground and then squashed with steel-toed boots. I was tempted to pull the alert chain but decided against it since it was too early to complain. Suddenly, the bathroom door opened and a short East Indian man, who was a male version of Nurse Priya with a Hitler-styled moustache, entered my quarters. Seeing me awake, he snapped to attention, placed his hands behind his back, bowed, and made his first words an apology and introduction:

"I am so sorry, Sir, for waking you. My name is Matt and I am your nurse."

I lifted an eyebrow and he shrugged as if to say, 'yes, can you believe it, a male nurse?'

"If you need anything to clean up or anything else please let me know."

I mentioned that I could care for myself, but he interjected:

"If you want to brush your teeth I can bring you toothpaste and water; if you want to sponge I can bring you a wet warm rag; if you want to release your bladder I can get you a pee container; if you want to brush your hair I can get you a comb." He stopped and looked at me sideways. "Wait what's wrong with you? Can you walk?" He didn't wait for a response. "You just tell me what you want and I will do it for you."

S.C.A.M. was the bomb! I was convinced that at a five star hotel wouldn't offer such services, but here was this tiny East Indian catering to my needs. For free? I hadn't planned on addressing my hygiene so early but decided that the nurse's proposals were too magnificent to ignore despite the coldness of the early hour. With astute decorum I indicated that a clean mouth, sponged skin and a release of the bladder were highly desired. I concurred:

"Yes, good Matt, bring me these things. Jolly good thank you."

In bootlicking fashion, he removed the required belongings from my bedside table then disappeared into the bathroom. I heard the tap flowing then a few seconds later he returned with a small bowl of water, a rag, a long-lipped container shaped like a juice mug and a toothbrush covered with toothpaste. He placed the items on the side table, stepped back and snapped to attention.

Looking at the countertop, I was at a loss. Was the bowl of water for me to moisten the rag or was it meant for washing my mouth? I looked at Matt to confirm, knowing very well that the *scoundrel* had seen through my *big shot* masquerading. He sheepishly indicated that the water in the bowl was for my mouth, and for the first time in my life I began brushing my teeth from bed. Then I needed to urinate. I grabbed the pee container, and after a confirming nod from Matt, stuck it under the sheet and between my legs, using my hands to guide my penis past the mummy wrappings to the mouth of the bottle. The first trickle soiled my hands and after some gentle readjustments I began the longest pee of my life; it was as if I had not micturated in days and instantly I regretted the aristocratic exploit I had undertaken. When I removed the apparatus, it was filled to the brim and for a second I swore that Nurse Matt's eyes nearly bulged from their sockets. When I clumsily attempted to pass the pee container along, he murmured adamantly in a thicker East Indian accent:

"Please... place it on the table."

Once I had applied the damp rag to my shoulders, neck, face and groin, he cautiously removed the dirty utensils individually, bearing an ill-disguised look which pronounced that he hated his job.

It was eight o'clock and I still had my two testicles.

Lasana's plan

Dissatisfied with my moist-rag bath, I checked the cross box; it was still there, undisturbed. Then for the first time, I noticed a clock above the entrance. I stared at the second hand in eager anticipation, knowing that any moment the doctor would visit his high-risk patient and bring to a close the entire ordeal. At eleven o'clock, no one had come except a nurse who introduced herself as Nurse Betty, Matt's replacement, in a solemn manner as if it were the changing of the guard. I felt sorely abandoned and wished to weep bitterly, but didn't. Instead, I opted to telephone my brother, Lasana, whose raucous voice greeted me on the other end of the line:

"One stones! Aye… boy, we going to cook that thing when you lose it right! How you think it go taste geera? *Nah*! I feel a curry stew is the real scene!"

I laughed out loud, prompting a streak of pain in my lower right stomach. I massaged the area and listened as he migrated to a more serious tone:

"Aye, Lyndon? Them people will rob you, boy. When they done with you, you have no stones and no money!"

To culminate the scenario, I mentioned that the doctor hadn't yet seen me for the morning despite the detrimental nature of my seeds. When he spoke again his voice was filled with aggression:

"You see them bastards how they is? Anyway boy, don't worry, I have a plan."

I groaned. My brother's plans, while comprehensive are usually chimeras, however, being desperate I listened. To give his plan credibility he retraced familiar ground and concluded:

"Dread, you need to get out of there or them people will rob you by the hour. That doctor just want you to stay in the room so he could make money and the place could make a thing on the side. You paying for every tablet, meal and balls inspection through your teeth. And at the end of it all you not even guaranteed to have two balls. Is better you let the government cut it off for free."

I saw the laughter on his face but his voice betrayed nothing.

"You need to get this surgery for free," he continued, "so hear what... I have a partner in Port of Spain General Hospital that working from four o'clock today. He says that he could get you admitted straight into Casualty."

The plan sounded excellent, causing me to nod positively.

"However, it have one problem," he said, and I stopped nodding and listened, "the problem is that you cannot be a walk-in patient. You have to arrive in an ambulance."

"Okay... but, Lasana, where the hell I getting an ambulance?" I cried.

"Boy, my partner Brigo! You know Brigo, right?

Right! He wife does drive ambulance. I could get she to pick you up."

I was way past beginning to doubt the plan. I lamented:

"Where she picking me up, Lasana? I not home, remember? I in a hospital!"

"Boy, don't study that! She will pick you up on the side of the road!" he reassured me.

"Boy, that plan real stupid," I stuttered crossly, maddened as my hopes had been quashed. "Can you imagine you and I parked on the side of the road looking like we in perfect health then an ambulance pulls up, I get in and then there are sirens blazing as they take me away? People will think you stab me in the front seat or something. That *rel* unrealistic!"

Apparently Lasana hadn't foreseen that scenario as there was silence and a quick goodbye followed by a click. But the telephone call had served as a transient saviour as I spent the next thirty minutes replaying it and laughing, oblivious to what would have otherwise been extreme pain.

Then Dr. Maharaj, *my* doctor, entered along with a nauseating odour of cigarette smoke. I wanted to reprimand him but instead dropped my pants on request, displaying my scrotums still wrapped like an Egyptian mummy. While he massaged my privates, again barehanded, he made comparisons between my right and left nut, and enquired of my night, symptoms of pain, times of severe attacks and so forth; I answered all honestly. With sudden somberness, he halted his inspection and lodged his elbows on the metal bars of the orthopaedic bed. An indefinite silence ensued, one in which I looked at him questioningly as he pondered long and hard. Finally, when the sudorific suspense climaxed, he admitted:

"I think we need to go in."

I understood perfectly, but replied:

"What?"

"I think… sorry, I know that we need to operate. I mean this is something which can reoccur anytime and anywhere. It is best we see about it immediately."

His voice never wavered. Perhaps it was because of my conversation with Lasana, but I now doubted how genuine Dr. Maharaj really was as he elaborated on all the right reasons to stitch my spermatic cord to the wall of my scrotums.

"So how much this entire procedure would cost, Doctor?" I was immediately disgusted by his answer:

"Oh I don't know as I don't get involved in that aspect of it. I simply do the surgery. You will have to ask the girls working here," he said, pointing to the silhouettes behind the door.

"But would you not be doing the operation?" I asked, thinking that Maharaj was too naïve to be a doctor since he was unaware of his services' costs. My tact earned me a price tag:

"Oh. It could be as *little* as twenty thousand dollars."

My testicles leaped into my stomach. However I managed to suppress a cough and kept a poker-straight face which pronounced that the money was at my fingertips.

"I'll need to discuss it with my family," I admitted coolly.

His eyes twinkled behind gilded spectacles.

"Your manhood is on the line here," he offered, "and if you don't do this now it will crop up at a later date. It's better that you get it over with."

Sensing a stratagem, I imposed:

"As I said, I'll have to discuss it with my family. The money is not a problem, but I do appreciate your advice." I smiled lamely, wishing I had a pot of leprechaun's gold to shower him with. "Thank you."

With an air of triumph he left, promising to return promptly, armed with a surgical proposal, but I felt certain that he was counting his chickens rather than tending to my eggs. When the doors swung shut, I dialled Lisa from my mobile telephone, low on battery life, and zealously updated her.

"Lyndon, you forget that, you hear me!" she said. "Lasana has a plan–" I groaned– "to get an ambulance to take you to the Port of Spain General Hospital."

"Why don't you come get me and take me down there? Lasana said that has to happen at four o'clock, it's now only–" I consulted the wall clock– "noon."

After some silence, she piped:

"Okay. I will be down there shortly as I have to talk to my supervisor but don't eat any food or take any medication, you hear me? They will bill you for it and as far as I concerned they already take a lot of *your* money."

She hung up.

Suddenly, Nurse Betty entered, trundling a food tray, a glass of juice and a cup of tablets even though my doctor had just recommended me for immediate surgery. I mentioned the impediment and she apologised profusely and wheeled the items out.

One hour later, Lisa arrived with an entourage: Uncle Ambrose, Aunt Betsy, Aunt Sylvia and Roxanne. The females all showered me with kisses and gracious, reassuring remarks then began inspecting the décor. My uncle, the businessman, slugged me a couple of low blows aimed directly and dangerously at my manhood. After his list of jests had been exhausted, he enquired about my financial status and medical insurance. I grimaced and waved a face-down palm. When everyone had settled and I was the centre of attention, a feeling of despair hovered. Sensing in my visitors a certain amount of enmity towards private health care, I spared no detail of my *horrid* experience thus far and exaggerated some. After my tantrum, Uncle Ambrose blatantly confessed:

"Yes! These people are sicker than their patients. Imagine I did some service for them a couple years ago. In fact they owe me a lot of money, over ten thousand dollars. They love to collect money but they don't like to pay out."

I wondered if there was anyway we could have filtered that money into my operation and call it square. He clasped the rails of the orthopaedic bed and twisted his face to match this sombre, salient point:

"Do you know that if a patient dies here the family is unable to reclaim the body until they have paid off all their expenses?"

Lisa gasped.

Aunt Betsy, the frank philanthropist, blurted:

"Oh-*gorm*, Ambrose! You serious?"

A lewd thought struck me:

"So wait, if my balls die and I don't pay the money you mean they will keep them?"

My aunts, seated in Gulliver's chair, scolded me while everyone else chuckled. Uncle Ambrose said:

"No, it's a serious thing. They will dig your eyes if you stay here any longer. Trust me, you better off going to General Hospital."

"So what do you think?" Lisa asked.

I contemplated the fiasco and admitted:

"Well… I have the money but no medical insurance. So should I decide to have the surgery my savings are damned. What do you think?" I directed the question to no one in particular.

"I believe that you should get the surgery done privately," said a skeptical Roxanne, "because there is also the crisis at the public hospital."

She lifted a newspaper which bore the bold caption: '*Patients sleep on the floor in San Fernando Hospital.*'

I was despondent about losing so much money *for just* one testicle and said so.

"Well, your best bet is the Port of Spain General Hospital," Lisa said and everyone except Roxanne agreed.

I was inclined to share my cousin's view but I caved in to the majority's vote. With the decision set in stone, all that was left was to be discharged. Up to that moment, I had always believed that someone could simply walk out of a hospital when they felt improved. Lisa left to oversee this and the rest of us engaged in small talk.

Some time later, Lisa returned with a sheet of paper as long as a Dead Sea scroll: it was my bill. From its length, one would have believed either that I had been at *S.C.A.M.* for weeks or I had been billed by the second. Lisa looked displeased and redder than usual as she stood by the door and vigorously waved the bill like a paper vendor.

"Can you believe these people?" she inveighed, twitching so violently that I feared she would pop her neck. "They are billing you for two nights and a single room!"

"But I haven't even been here for a day! Right? However, I am in a single room," I observed.

Uncle Ambrose fumed:

"These people are sick, I tell you! I telling you is over twenty thousand dollars they owe me!"

Lisa continued exasperatedly:

"When I had booked you, I requested a ward with three other patients but as none was available they placed you in here. I'm not taking this *stupidness*, you hear? Humph! Nonsense! Nonsense!"

A gorgeous, well-dressed African lady with an air of alacrity entered the room with humble apologies for encroaching. Immediately, she and my sister engaged in a diplomatic yet seemingly heated conversation regarding the bill. Lisa pointed to various line items as she spoke:

"Yes! You see here, on this line, it says *by* two nights. Mind you, my brother only stayed here one. And this detail here… where is it? Oh yes! Here it is… it says that the payment is for a single room and not a ward as was requested. You all will need to adjust that since *S.C.A.M.* had no rooms available. And this eighteen hundred dollars here… yes, the one for a blood test and the eight hundred and fifty dollars for medication… I would like a line-by-line breakdown of that please. Thank you very much!"

Lisa smirked at the *S.C.A.M.* employee who looked

like she had been struck by a meteor. Without a word the woman left, fluttering the bill as if it was utter nonsense to have burdened us with such inaccuracies. When the doors swung shut, Uncle Ambrose huffed:

"You see what I mean? They sick! I telling you that is over thirty thousand dollars they have for me!"

I thought: maybe he was accruing interest each time he recapped the total. Lisa on the other hand was flushed. She trembled angrily, hers lips quivered, she vigorously batted her eyelids, and I thought she looked like a purple, epileptic dinosaur. She shook her head and waved outward palms in true Lisa fashion, declaiming:

"Real nonsense, I tell you! They are fleecing poor people out of their money!"

I gently reminded her that the poverty-stricken couldn't pay the initial fee, and I had chosen to be admitted as a desperate resort. Only then did she calm down. We waited for over one hour until the accountant returned with the adjusted bill then disappeared before my sister could inspect it. Lisa piped:

"But wait! Where the doctor?" The diplomacy in her voice was gone. "Is over ah hour and ah half I ask for you to be discharged and he not here yet? Like they really want to keep you long enough to bill you for two days?"

She excused herself and returned minutes later, still simmering in clammy exasperation. She revealed that Dr. Maharaj was writing a procedure – at least it was what the administrative staff had said, she shrugged.

"What is a procedure?" I asked, but no one knew so talk reverted to why the doctor was slighting his prized patient.

Aunt Sylvia, an incessant purist and Roxanne's mother, spoke for the first time:

"Lisa, you must remember that this gentleman is a doctor who has other patients."

She was a nurse also and therefore understood the nature of the work more than I cared to at that point in time, but being the eldest of our aunts, we remained silent even though the mark of dissent was crudely painted on Lisa's face; mine too.

A long time passed and still no Dr. Maharaj; those were interminable minutes. I resolved to make the situation *appear* serious to the jokers outside so, despite my pain, I donned shoes and jeans and stepped outside to where six females were cramped behind a tiny area designed to seat three. I leaned on the counter and, uncertain how to begin, stood while they froze. I decided on the painfully polite approach:

"Um… I'm not usually a fussy person, but I am in a lot of pain. My stones are really hurting and I will like to be discharged from this place. Can you please help me?"

No one giggled and a surfeit of hands concurrently shot towards the telephone receiver. One won and after quick stabs at small, worn-out knobs, an inaudible conversation followed. The call ended and collectively they all assured me that the doctor would arrive in fifteen minutes. I returned to my room and Dr. Maharaj appeared in five, reeking of cigarette smoke. He navigated through my visitors' legs until he came to my bedside, where I waited, praying that I wouldn't have to *drop 'em* one more time. He queried my decision and although I was inclined to reprimand his negligence, I figured that it was safer to say nothing, as he and I might do business again in the near or distant future. With monumental conviction, I repeated my rehearsed and final decision and, strangely, he never cajoled me to commit to the twenty-thousand-dollar surgery. At that time, I was certain he felt condemned about how he had acted and, without further ado, he hand-delivered a discharge form.

Then, he and Lisa left to tally *his* bill.

The strain of the morn's events had worn me thin and riddled me with a pain which knotted itself into tight metal balls, vibrating violently and exploding in my lower stomach. I wished it away and, thankfully, Aunt Sylvia had pain killers. Aunt Betsy hadn't stopped talking since Lisa had left the room, and was making plans to stay behind for support. When Lisa returned, she rolled her eyes and celebrated that the bills had been paid, and I was free to go.

I rolled out of the orthopaedic bed, like a shell-shocked veteran and, like a cowboy, ambled out of Ward Seven. Immediately, a support staff, identifiable by his brown garb, stopped me and pointed to the wheelchair. I protested; I wanted to walk out of the institution, but the head nurse ordered me to sit while the same nurses whom I had politely approached smiled with approval. At least she cared about me, I thought, doing as instructed and the support staff member, a dignified wheelchair driver, whisked me away from Ward Seven.

Outside the nursing home, I was stationed atop the ramp, while Lisa was instructed to fetch her vehicle. Everyone, except Aunt Betsy and a nurse who had joined us, left my side. From where I sat, I observed a man in the driveway, pleading with another nurse for a wheelchair to carry a sick woman slouched over in the front seat of an idling van. The nurse indicated that there was none, but I shouted that they could use mine. The nurse standing next to me ordered me to stay, like a dog, as I had already paid for the chair. I couldn't believe it! I had been misled. The head nurse hadn't cared one farthing when she had convinced me to sit due to my excruciating pain; it was merely because I had *a'ready paid* for the service. I rose from the wheelchair and stated:

"Most times it isn't about the money. It's about making sacrifices to help people who are sick regardless of the price attached to it."

She twisted her face and left, but I was happy. It remains a factor of the capitalist order which I detest: private healthcare. With that done, I walked laboriously to the car park, hand-in-hand with Aunt Betsy, renewed, but grossly unprepared for my next destination.

The time was unknown but I still had my two testicles.

Port of Spain General Hospital

◇◇

I basked in silence during the fifteen-minute drive to the public hospital, not in the mood for chitchat, a feeling I left unvoiced as I endured the high-pitched pampering of Aunt Betsy and Lisa.

The hospital was an edifice of old English architecture designed with a myriad of alcoves from which an army of solemn faces appeared and disappeared abruptly, like ants clambering to and fro an anthill. Aunt Betsy and I exited the car, and I watched Lisa leave to find a park, gravely hoping that she wouldn't be long in coming. In the past few hours she had unknowingly become my stronghold and now, with her gone, I felt naked; but waiting wasn't an option.

Aunt Betsy and I entered A & E.

Perhaps the stink of a sick bay is ecumenical: that immediate stench of rarefied, impenetrable doom which summons brief hesitation to the strides of the inflicted and forces them to shut their eyes, inhale quickly, exhale loudly through dime-sized mouths, blink rapidly, hold their breath and lurch forward with eyes fastened to the floor because they are afraid to see the faces of others; scared, because they do not wish to confirm that someone might be suffering more than they themselves. I walked with my back erect, head tipped forward and eyes downwards to an available seat adjacent to the receptionist's desk, protected by an immense window, like the ones which shield cashiers at multinational corporations, and an innumerable amount of burglar proofing that extended to the ceiling. No one was behind the stronghold. I exhaled, inhaled and tasted each nameless epidemic. Then, God sent someone; a big-bellied security guard appeared behind the steel gate, pointed at me and demanded in a thunderous but innocuous manner:

"You there! What's your problem?"

I still didn't know how to answer the question. I grimaced and pointed to my groin repeatedly as I craftily glanced at other patients from the corner of my eyes. The guard understood and beckoned that Aunt Betsy should bring my documents to him. Then he disappeared ephemerally. He flung open the gate and instructed me to follow arrows which formed a path.

"You have been marked as red," he said ominously, as I walked past.

I looked back, but Lisa hadn't yet come and I grieved that I would never see a familiar face again. With a sad smile, I waved at Aunt Betsy.

The heart of A & E is life on an alien world; I was inside the anthill. I robotically followed tiny, carmine arrows, spaced every three feet, gradually veering to the right of the vast enclosure and away from green arrows which led in the opposite direction. I wondered about the magnitude of difference in the level of suffering between persons marked as red versus green. Patients were everywhere: lulled off on stretchers, beds, chairs and ottomans scattered and crammed into every nook. Doctors and nurses bustled and shouted at each other in unfamiliar accents and argots. The doctors were tall, like giants, and had faces of despots. Nigerians, I figured. The nurses were short, beautiful, Asian women who were so petite that they appeared to meet these white-robed, African physicians at their waists.

The red arrows stopped in an area adorned with ruffled beds and tattered blinds, and three young chaps who might have been interns waved me over to a cubicle in the far corner. I lay on a stretcher as they tightly wrapped a pressure band around my flaccid bicep. The tallest then asked me the standard list of questions which I had long memorised, while the shortest scribbled my hurried answers. The pressure gauge beeped and displayed figures. The chap who did nothing whistled:

"*Whey Sah*! Pressure for so!"

Not a good sign, I figured, but thought little of it as they hurried away to summon a doctor.

A patient was admitted to the bed nearest me and dismal, blue blinds were jangled shut, but a shotgun-sized hole revealed the clandestine activities. Sickened, yet entranced by the macabre ordeal, I watched as needles repeatedly punctured the patient's hands and legs… then blood boiled from the wounds. There was endless silence, then a long, monotone beep erupted. I had seen and felt everything which occurred. Devastated, I looked away.

A doctor the height of a lamppost popped into the cubicle where I lay. He had a mean face that held a pudgy nose tucked beneath fierce eyes, and ears as large as wine corks. His hands were on his waist and his fingers were stuck into the front pockets of his soiled, white coverall. He reeked of the same urgency which torments one who must save the world, and when he spoke his voice boomed.

"What?" I asked with a twisted face. I had heard: '*Ah-boo-magadoobar!*'

Apparently he had spoken in his native tongue but chose not to surrender this information.

"I asked you why you are here."

Instantly, I disliked him but still I shared my crisis.

"Take off your pants. I will be right back."

He left the blinds spread apart but I wasn't about to give a free show. I shut the curtains, staying clear of all holes, undressed and stood stark naked with my testicles hanging a bit lower than they usually did. Doctor Giant returned, wearing gloves as I wasn't paying him huge amounts to feel my nuts barehanded. He squeezed, he touched, he compared, squeezed some more then grunted:

"This isn't testicular torsion. If it was, you would have already lost the testicle."

What the hell? Why could no one agree? Why was he speaking of my ball so casually in Casualty? In cricket it's called *lost ball win*.

"You have to do a blood and urine test," he said sharply.

I mentioned that I already had the results for these tests in my pocket. The doctor looked at me from head to toe with contempt, as if I reminded him of the apartheid system, and barked:

"No! You do it here," pointing to the floor, like I had to pee on that exact spot. He produced an iridescent pallet and pointed to the toilet, tapping the coloured bit of wood against his waist. He commanded: "Go there and pee on this stick! Make sure it flows down this path! When you are finished, return here and lie down so we can take your blood."

I did as he had instructed and another doctor came to my bedside. He was as tall as the first, had a sparkling baldhead, glasses of a scholar and smooth cocoa features which would have looked good on a girl. He spoke in a slow, controlled voice:

"Good day, Sir. I am here to take your blood. Can you please pull up your jersey?"

I did so hesitantly and he promptly wrapped a surgical glove around my bicep, a primitive yet effective technique since my veins began bulging. He vigorously tapped my arms to hasten the bloating, then suddenly, without any warning, began thrusting the needle into my arm.

"You have small veins for a big man," he noted, after failing to locate one.

I was uncertain that it was a compliment so said nothing. Finally, it was over and I opened my eyes in relief, but the doctor was pricking the needle repeatedly into my wrist. Finally, he stopped and after some fussing, I noticed the little, blue device he had attached to my forearm, just below the palm. I could cue the rigid impression of a three-inch-long needle forced upwards against my skin. I began sweating profusely. I felt faint.

I fussed, sliding my feet up and about. I dangerously arched my back and groaned loudly, as if I had fallen from a tree. I begged for water. The doctor left and I never saw him again.

Sometime after I had consoled myself, I saw a familiar doctor: it was Lasana's friend, and because it was expected that I should know his name, he neglected to introduce himself. He mentioned that I would be taken to Ward Twenty-one, then to surgery since I had torsion and my right testicle was threatened. I wondered which doctor had made the right diagnosis: was it Lasana's friend, Dr. Narine, Dr. Maharaj or the Nigerian? When he was finished, two support staff appeared and helped me onto a stretcher, then they, along with a nurse, began wheeling me to Ward Twenty-one.

On the way I saw visitors, patients, more Nigerian doctors and Asian nurses, but saw no one I knew except for Doctor Gorilla from *Special Care Associates of Medicine*. How peculiar it was to see a man who had felt my testicles, I thought, and wondered why he, a privately employed doctor, was working at a public institution. I waved but he looked away; perhaps he hadn't recognised me.

At least I still had my two testicles.

Ward 21

◇◇◇◇◇◇◇◇◇

Ward Twenty-one, the surgical ward, was at the pinnacle of one of the minarets in the eastern block. It was a capacious, neat room with a myriad of beds which lacked patients, as if everyone was in surgery. Protocol defines that a nurse must admit a patient to a ward, thus revealing the purpose of the lady who had walked with us from A & E. Once admitted, I moved from the stretcher to a semi-soft, semi-comfortable bed with spotless, white sheets. A male nurse appeared, crudely manipulated some knobs on the bed's control panel and the backrest magically jerked into an upright position. Once he had demonstrated the function of each button, he thought it necessary to crack a humourless joke about my testicles and left before I could retort.

A stunning, young doctor with a shock of black hair appeared shortly after and pulled the curtains around the bed. It was time; before she asked, I *dropped them* and lay down. A male and female nurse appeared while this doctor fondled my jewels, the right one a dazzling ruby. For the first time, I didn't close my eyes but instead focussed intensely on the male nurse, the same one who had previously joked with me, as he uncomfortably stood witness to the spectacle. His eyes shifted from the ceiling to the doctor to my scrotums, still bandaged and shrivelled. Each time our eyes met, I smiled broadly as if to say, *got you*, and only now, as I write this, does it strike me that he probably figured me for a homosexual. Absolutely hilarious! After awhile, the confused, callow doctor instructed me to zip up and left with the female nurse and a happy Adrian, such being his name. Without warning, the physician returned with an immense Nigerian co-worker who looked expensive to feed. He had a fat face which bore a scruffy beard and moustache.

"Do you want to drop your pants for me?" he asked politely, as if I could refuse.

I said no for the heck of it, but slid my pants off. He felt around gingerly, teasing my testicles with his index finger and finally exclaimed:

"Yes! Indeed! This is testicular torsion! You need to have surgery right away!"

Seemingly excited at the prospect, they left me with my pants down. When they didn't return, I dressed and stared at the four curtains blanketing me, wondering how he and Dr. Giant, two doctors of the same race, from the same country and same institution, could make vastly differing diagnoses.

Without warning, not one, two or three but eight doctors stormed into my pen and surrounded my bed like excited archaeologists who had just come across the remains of the earliest man. It was a cosmopolitan set of youths who struck me as too inexperienced and cheery to be doctors or surgeons, but they were dressed the role, so I guessed: interns. The one to my left, a petite East Indian girl, spoke bravely on behalf of the others:

"Hi! We are all student doctors and we have heard that you have this problem which we would like to talk to you about. Is this okay with you?"

I depressed the control on my bed until I was erect and ascertained each face, wondering who would be the bravest to request an inspection. Even the only male in the group looked like a girl with his shoulder-length hair. I nodded okay. The fair-skinned intern with short, rusty hair spoke:

"We understand you have a condition known as testicular torsion and it's quite an uncommon event. Have you ever heard about it before?"

"Before Monday… no," I admitted.

The male piped:

"Do you know what you have?"

Every group has a bore and because the African student adjacent to him rolled her eyes, I entertained him: 'testicular torsion.'

An African girl, opposite the tiny intern, asked:

"So what symptoms did you notice or feel before the event?"

"Nothing! It occurred without warning as I was painting." Then I rubbed my skin and declared, "Not even a fever, even though it is one of the symptoms."

"What exactly do you know about your condition?" the petite East Indian enquired.

I decided to go for the long haul:

"The bell clapper deformity is one whereby a few males may have an abnormally longer spermatic cord than others. As a result this can twist easier causing a kink which locks off the blood supply, thereby killing the testes within minutes if not corrected… a fixation means that this same cord must be shortened by suturing it to the walls of the scrotum."

The fair-skinned trainee looked impressed and said so. I nodded a thank you and the impaired student broke the silence:

"So you notice any symptoms, like fever or anything?"

The same African intern nudged him sharply with her elbow. Then the compartment was engulfed in silence. Almost as if on cue, the huge Nigerian returned and began interrogating his minions. He looked at me and, to my disbelief, casually enquired:

"So! You want to show it to them?"

"Anything for academics," I blurted and lurched from the bed.

My pants came off first, then my boxers. The bandage had unstuck and now dangled around my balls like tassels. Male ego stepped in and I was disappointed at my manhood, a flaccid elephant trunk and battered table tennis balls which had been mashed, boiled, abused and boiled again.

"Do you want to feel it too?" I asked, displaying the spectacle to the room by grinding my waist in a semicircle; only the bandage was large enough to flutter.

Almost without hesitation, although this may have been my egoistic analysis, the petite East Indian produced gloves from her coverall and slipped them on with a loud smack. Then, she proceeded to squeeze.

When the students had huddled closer, the Nigerian said in his thick, sonorous accent:

"As you all can *seeeeeeee* the right testicle is a bit *swollennnnnnn* and *reddddddddddd.*"

The male intern interjected:

"What if his testicles are naturally big and red?"

No answer was warranted so the ring master continued:

"If you feel closer to the top right of the testicle you will notice that the spermatic cord feels a bit swollen."

The gloved intern followed the doctor's voice to the spot and confirmed that *it* felt *huge* in her hands. A few students giggled at the pun and one nearly fell on me; I myself laughed. Sensing that the tutorial had become a fiasco, the big man closed the session and one-by-one the interns left with best of wishes. I joked that I hoped the next time I saw them I still had my two testicles. Feeling somewhat relaxed, I closed my eyes.

I hadn't been asleep for long because when I awoke the outside world revealed sunshine as brilliant as when I had been admitted to Surgical. I yelped in happiness. Lisa and Aunt Betsy had found me! And I am still shocked that they did, especially after I had disappeared into A & E and had been trundled through a hopeless-to-memorise labyrinth of corridors. They whispered that the doctor had ordered a switch to Ward Twelve and although I had no idea what *Urology* meant, I neglected to ask, since word in no way sounded threatening. Then, the gentlemen who had brought me to Ward Twenty-one appeared with a rickety stretcher and whisked me away to Ward Twelve.

My two testicles vibrated during the entire ride.

Urology

◇◇◇◇◇◇◇◇◇◇

Urology was two stories down (I believe) and lacked neither patients nor nurses. I was shoved into a dismal, dispiriting corner where a conspicuous figure six was plastered midway up the opposite wall. What were the odds of striking six three times? *666*! I knew this was the mark of the beast but was too weary at the time to pay any attention to such superficial superstitions which I would have otherwise regarded as inauspicious. Slot number six was yards away from other patients, an observation which prompted me to wonder whether the area was reserved for those plagued with communicable diseases, and directly next to shutters adjacent to the outside corridor. Because visiting hours were long over, my guests stood in the wide walkway, peeping through the window, to the overt disgust of the nurses who stood conspiring something or the other around a large desk. The needle in my hand was driving me insane and I began to sweat profusely, worse than I did in A & E. Lisa, pallid from the imbroglio, interceded:

"Oh gosh, nurse, we didn't bring this boy here to die. Is only a little testicles problem he have."

Behind the desk, a nurse with a weave thicker than a horse's mane, pointed angrily at the crowd outside and blustered:

"People! You are distracting my patient! If you want to stay there, don't arouse him!"

Little did she know that I couldn't be aroused, not even by a stampede. Not wanting to perturb my guardians, I quietly but reluctantly requested that Lisa and company leave. They did and for the second time I was alone, scared and solitary with a spectacular, southern view of the capital which failed to appeal.

I began losing track of time and an eerie darkness crept over the vast sea of concrete outside my window and bit-by-bit each ward was ghostly illuminated. Without warning, screams would resonate through the vast expanse then ebb to an agonising gurgle. At other times, shrill sirens would pierce the heaviness of the impenetrable night and metal gratings would clank as unseen ambulances sped away to fetch the dying or perhaps return with the already dead. Throughout my stay, these noises would continue to chill my bones to brittleness.

My solace was a pinnacle atop a church, set on a distant hill, in an area I believed and later confirmed to be Laventille; in it I found quietness and a distraction as time crawled by and the patients in Urology, somewhere aft of me, added to the hospital's howls. What might have been hours later, I was still anxiously awaiting surgery and so hadn't yet eaten.

The specialist appeared on the ward sometime after

the daily news programme which reverberated from a patient's radio, suggesting that it was about seven o'clock. She looked local and had uptight, sinister features as if vexed with something or someone. As soon as she faded into the depths of Ward Twelve, patients began screaming in amplified tones. I was horrified. Was she here to torture me? I waited, determined not to receive attention if proffered but after dozens of heated wails, she appeared at my bedside. Without pleasantries, she told me to reveal my testicles, and I did, but shielded my healthy ball, a movement which puffed my right red nut.

"Move your hands them," she chided. She spoke like a Trinidadian who had studied at Oxford University and had maintained the English drawl, but hadn't shed the green verbs consistent with island dialect.

I did and she poked around a bit. Suddenly, she sneezed. She sneezed again and again. She sacrificed etiquette for performance, her hands crushing my testicles with each gush of wet exhaust that sprinkled my groin. Why didn't she cover her mouth? I protested incoherently because I feared her deeply. Then she left and I hoped that there were no diseases transferable via spittle on the testicles. She disappeared behind the counter and after some thumping of numbers on a telephone atop the desk, sat and spoke inaudibly for a few minutes. Once finished, she returned and sullenly gave the okay; I could eat as there would be no surgery. However, I was to apply ice to the area to aid blood circulation. She departed again, seemingly disappointed that I hadn't screamed once throughout the entire procedure.

Suddenly, I realised how famished I truly was. My

stomach growled and somersaulted again and again, as I failed to harness the attention of the many nurses, who still somberly patrolled the ward. Nurses are strange, I thought, as I watched them. While they were dedicated, smart individuals who had committed their lives to saving people most did so in a stringent manner which lacked the care and love that sick people yearn. The harshness with which they addressed the unwell certainly led me to believe so. They seemed only polite to the doctors who they appeared to cower before, like servants before a fastidious master. Finally one, on her eleventh walk past me, came and spoke urgently, almost as if someone was dying just down the hall and she was the key to their survival:

"Yes! What you want?"

"Nurse, pardon me, but I real hungry," I said, patting my stomach.

"That is all? The kitchen closed!" she replied, then stormed off.

I focussed on the pinnacle in the distance and found temporary mental comfort which didn't ease my physical pain or that of the others who groaned, moaned and beseeched God for relief. I felt death would have been more welcome than being in this antiseptic hell. Of course, I was several stories up and the rampart outside was low enough for a suicidal patient to leap over and plunge to doom. I shuddered at the devilish thought and wondered how many suicides had occurred at the hospital; the direct result of despair, pain, hopelessness and the unwillingness of the mind to live although the body wasn't yet dead.

In time, the uptight nurse reappeared carrying a

small, blue, plastic plate filled with two slices of bread and a few sausages, and a humongous mug topped with a hot, brown drink, lurking layers of steam dancing from its brim. Instantly my despair vanished. She placed the goodies on a side table and laboriously adjusted it until it was an appropriate height to pass over the bed. I thanked her profusely and this time a pleasant smile crossed her face; after an almost imperceptible hesitation, she left.

I whispered a brief prayer then ardently dug into the meal. Immediately, all my fears of hospital food, instilled by wandering, atavistic stories, were vanquished. The cup of cocoa truly cheered my heart for when it settled in my stomach I became submerged in fields of gold with a loved one, running barefooted as birds whistled melodious Psalms. To this day, it remains the most superb cup of cocoa I ever drank [*and I have modified this line, years later, to reinforce the point*]. It was also the largest and for that I was grateful. I fell asleep that night, knowing that I had breakfast to look forward to and I trusted that the plan included cocoa.

A wrenching pain jolted me awake at a time I cannot recall. Was I at home? Blast it! I was also unaware of the date and how long I had been in hospital. I glanced downwards and stifled a howl when I saw the projection of the needle, embedded in my wrist. I must have made a noise because a young male doctor, dressed like a butcher, came running. He looked and spoke like a baddie from an old Chinese kung fu flick; obviously, he had learnt English in the wrong place.

"What the mata with you? What the mata?"

As I would learn, he stretched each word with two or

more syllables, or every third word. I wiggled to exaggerate my pain then whimpered about the discomfort in my wrist.

"Oh that? I dunno why them fellaz from Cazualtee like do that. It more beta they put it here," he said, slapping above his knuckles to indicate the spot. "Wat hand you wite with?"

I offered my right hand. He motioned for me to wait then quickly left and returned with another syringe, cotton and an alcohol-based solution. I closed my eyes and squirmed as he did his job. I was still dancing in bed when I heard him say:

"Wat you doing dat for? I finish long time! You a big man, behave like one nuh."

Surprised, I looked down. The blue-capped device was on my left hand just above the knuckles and the other that had been appended to my wrist was gone. I folded and unfolded the now burdened left hand and to my great delight felt little pain and saw no metallic projections against my skin. I thanked him and without any acknowledgement he rattled off machine gun English which I needed subtitles to understand. After the lecture, I was confused and he looked exasperated. He waved wildly in the air, completing what looked like a karate skit, then left. When he returned he had bandages and a surgical glove, filled with a surfeit of cold water and ice, and knotted at its base. He spoke slowly and lifted the items, pointing where necessary so I could connect the dots:

"Icepack! *Bandlage*! Balls! I wrap. Then we put ice. You need to ice the spot to encourage *circuation*. I need you to take down…"

I interjected:

"But isn't my problem also known as *winter syndrome*?" Wouldn't gloves filled with ice worsen the situation?"

His face flared with anger and not wanting to risk another karate demonstration, I dropped my pants and he began wrapping me with his bare hands, like Dr. Maharaj had at *Special Care Associates of Medicine*. I was conscious and ashamed of my scent since my last bath had been ages ago at the private facility. While he wrapped around legs and balls, he confirmed, in abrupt sentences, that the other doctors firmly believed that I didn't have a torsion (which he pronounced '*tersian*') but an infection with similar symptoms. In light of this conjecture, I was to be placed on antibiotics and closely monitored for a few days. When the doctor was finished everything but my testicles were supported. Then he placed the cold, long-fingered surgical-gloves-turned-icepack onto my shrivelled seeds. I drifted into a disturbed sleep just as he was slipping a long tube into the uncapped apparatus on my left hand.

I awoke when the pink rays of the morn's light had just begun flanking the grey darkness of the night. My bed was drenched and I immediately grabbed for my crotch to see if the icepack had burst. The glove was intact but filled with warm water.

I needed a bath. I looked over the side of the bed trying to gauge the cleanliness of the floor and unable to tell, experienced the gush of renewed frustration; I had no slippers. I inhaled deeply, attempting to sniff the floor, and waves of disinfectant and other revolting hospital scents withered my initial inclination to set my feet down. However, the urgency with which I desired cleanliness compelled me to gather clean clothes and towel from my pauper's bag.

Then, I began my bare-soled journey across the floor.

To get to the bathroom, I had to walk deeper into Urology, past the other patients whom I had never seen. The aisle was walled with beds on either side and bore gentlemen predominantly of the African race. Inert faces acknowledged me briefly and returned to their despair. Some of the men were uncovered and lay staring at their crotches which bore threatening catheters that led to bags, hooked to the bedsides, filled with a distasteful mix of urine and blood. The word *Uro*logy suddenly made sense and quickly I wobbled to the bathroom. At the doorway, a nurse with a quick stride chastised me for not wearing slippers.

The bathroom was surprisingly clean with a column of tiny showers lined up like soldiers. Each unit was adorned with a diaphanous flower-patterned, plastic curtain, and while it endorsed privacy, I didn't wish it to caress me, so I showered exposed to other early-bird patients who came to brush their teeth or release their burdened bowels. Randomly, nurses entered to ensure the well-being of their patients. I remained encased beneath the hot shower for a long spell (clenching my buttocks each time someone passed) in a futile attempt to cleanse my worries and diminish my pain. I stopped only when another patient haughtily exclaimed that he had waited long enough, even though upon my exit I noticed that the adjacent showers were empty.

Refreshed, I returned to bed, greeting more of the

sick during the slow walk and vainly anticipating the horde of expected visitors. Eva arrived, armed with a sandwich wrapped in foil, at the moment the Asian doctor was addressing the morning shift of nurses who were all taller than him. I brought Eva up to date on the cocoa, the fact that hospital food was quite palatable, the midnight screams, the sorry patients who had catheters inserted into their penises, and the crude icepacks. When she left, I half-heartedly indulged in the sandwich and looked around at the busied nurses who had files crudely labelled with scotch tape bearing numbers that had been retraced countless times. Like worker ants gathering food, the nurses followed invisible lines to corresponding patients. I anxiously kept watch but never saw a folder marked *Six*.

Eventually, a thin-as-a-toothpick nurse with a lovely brown complexion, baby bird features, and a lock of hair that fell over her eye, approached my bed. She had slipped past the curtain which shielded the patient behind me, armed with two maroon folders containing a surfeit of documents. She introduced herself as Nurse George and enquired of my night, the food, how I felt about the treatment and whether or not I needed anything. After a slow silence and the reluctant shake of my head, she notified me that another patient was being discharged and I would take his spot in the heart of the ward, a promise which I hoped would be broken.

When breakfast with another fantastic cup of cocoa was finished, two support staff showed and, acting upon strict instructions from the head nurse, shuttled Patient Six to the vacant slot fifteen, indeed in the heart of the ward. Nurse George appeared promptly (I was still

Patient Six according to the folder) and administered the morning dose of antibiotics through the syringe in my knuckles, the result of which prompted a numbing sting that snaked violently up my hand. She left without apology.

I scanned the heart of Urology, flicking my hand to earn release. With my head glued to the pillow, I crooked to the right: there was a patient between the window and I, but I couldn't see his face as a sea of nurses and a doctor had him encircled. I heard the physician saying:

"Mr. Thomas, do you have any friends whom you can get blood from? You need five pints and as you do know you have only two."

At the word blood, I looked to my left. An elderly East Indian lay two paces away, stricken by the unforgiving rancour of prostate cancer which had rendered his sheets bloody. A catheter was quickly depositing blood into a bag hooked to his bed, which had been adjusted so that the upper half was angled acutely in what must have been an uncomfortable position. Yet, he bore the serene finish of a philanthropist, a man who feared neither life nor destiny. Our eyes made four and he initiated a quiet conversation that lasted for a long time. His soft words confirmed my initial opinion. His name was Mr. Deonarine and speaking to him was like relating to my paternal or maternal grandfather of whom I have little or no memories.

"Son," he whispered gravely at one point and fell asleep midsentence.

Across the room were three beds that formed precise rows with Mr. Thomas', mine and Mr. Deonarine's. The one closest to the window bore an old East Indian who looked like a baby vulture that had a few strands of grey poking out of its bald crown like thistles. He had a visitor, an attractive girl who looked old enough to be his daughter but too young to be his wife. My glances caught their attention and we acknowledged greetings via waves and bobbing heads. They exchanged words, pointed at me and after awkward smiles, my eyes drifted left.

The patient in the middle, to your consternation, would become my favourite, an archaic, decrepit gent, showing lacerations specific to old age. He might have been blind and his mouth would always be opened each time I set furtive stares upon him. Mr. Alexander might have been a century old but looked more like a relic of the hospital, a permanent fixture which had existed since time itself. For the duration of my stay, various nurses would attend to this inconsolable man morning, noon and night, and cajole him to eat spoonfuls of a purple paste which I reckoned was unpalatable. In his bad moments, which included each spoonful to his lips, he caterwauled in a continuous, monotonic shriek:

"Oh-gawd-oh-gawd-oh-gawd-oh-gawd!"

At that moment the nurse who was feeding him scolded Mr. Alexander with admirable calmness and in the harmonious voice of an expert choirgirl. To this day, my imagination is unable to shape any conclusion which depicts the experiences which might have conditioned Mr. Alexander to scream at the sense of touch, and I wonder how often he had misjudged the intention of the nurses' fingers that compassionately stroked his side and gingerly wiped smudges of food from his chin. Throughout my stay, he would have no visitors but would retain an army of attentive, young women who diligently assumed the role of caring daughters. [*However, two months after I had been discharged, I visited Urology only to discover that location number twelve was vacant and there was absolutely no evidence that Mr. Alexander, Mr. Deonarine, Mr. Thomas and The man in a lot of pain – like myself – had ever existed in Ward Twenty-one. When I enquired, a nurse clad in a baby-blue pinafore, the same one who had fed me my first meal, simply shrugged, smiled, and resumed the long, arduous swipes of her mop as if she were the one erasing the memories.*]

To Mr. Alexander's right was another inconsolable patient who had been gripped by some insidious illness which, because of fear, I never queried. Without warning, he would offer the scream of the demented and impetuously contort into a fetal position and remain inflexible for minutes at a time, perhaps in vain attempts to lighten his pain by torturing other body parts. When his pain was especially severe, he muttered incoherently, howled and squirmed, and this he did continuously. I was overwhelmingly sorry for him but wished none of his agony, dubbing him *The man in a lot of pain.*

Beyond *this man* was a corridor that led to the bathroom and other wards. But, a daisy chain of frosty curtains hid the patients beyond the aisle, although someone's radio was always audible and kept me in touch with the hour, yet somehow when it mattered least.

After Mr. Thomas had been attended to, I, Patient Six, who had assumed Location Fifteen, was visited by a horde of nurses who enveloped my bedside along with a suave, inimitable Nigerian doctor.

"And who is this?" he asked the only nurse who wore white garbs.

"Patient Six," she responded.

I had always thought that prisoners alone were directly identified by numbers; perhaps she knew I didn't wish to be in Urology and so had qualified me as a convict.

"Oh, it is you!"

He smiled slyly with the nurses as if they were about to enjoy a treat at my expense. Without warning, his hands gestured with the mocking finesse of an eccentric musical conductor:

"Please, please, please! Pull the curtains."

In lighting moves I was boxed off and faces huddled over.

"Can we see the spot please?" he asked in his honey-coated voice, accompanied by *the* dazzling ivory smile of smiles.

I complied, my eyes closed in utmost embarrassment.

"Wait... what is this?" he asked.

I opened my eyes and braced for an imminent joke in the company of nurses.

"Who made this wrap?" the Nigerian demanded.

The head nurse held her right palm facedown, about five feet off the floor, and the same height of her breasts, a simple move which betrayed the apparent wrongdoing of the Asian doctor who had attended to me the night before. The Nigerian sighed sharply:

"This is not a wrap! This is a tourniquet!" With a mischievous whisper he asked, "Are we trying to kill this young man's testicles?"

A few of the nurses giggled. Then, in a more serious accent, he instructed:

"You will rewrap this *specimen* and add more ice to

the patient." Then he looked at me, slapped my shoulders heartily like I was someone he had met at a party, and with a wink exclaimed, "She will give you a wrap like you have never had before!"

The nurses giggled again at his drollery.

Then, a remarkable thing happened, something which was revealed to me only after contemplation. The jester indiscernibly transitioned into a meticulous doctor and catechised my problem from its onset: the hopeless painting, the interminable wait at Mount Hope, my brief occupation at *S.C.A.M.* and, finally, my admission at the General Hospital. I quickly recounted the more pertinent details while he listened with knitted eyebrows and a slow bobbing head. When I disclosed the cost of the proposed surgery at *S.C.A.M.*, he crossly announced:

"Can you imagine that? Imagine paying $20,000.00 for a surgery that would have taken no more than five minutes. Oh the poor of this country will suffer! Yes, Sir, poor people will suffer!" But his eyes twinkled when he concluded, "You, however, my dear friend, may very well be discharged tomorrow."

After he had gone to Patient Twelve, I reflected on the doctor's high level of interpersonal skills, the light moments that had carved a propitious setting and cushioned the heaviness when I spoke of my illness. Secretly, and unwisely, as his amiable personality held preponderance over his hidden skills, I hoped that should my testicles ever require suturing that the Nigerian Casanova would be the surgeon. The curtains engulfed Mr. Alexander and a glut of screams erupted, not comical as they often appeared due to his legendary proclivity to outbursts but rather howls that shattered the mind's shield of sanity:

"Oh-gawd-oh-gawd-oh-gawd-oh-gawd!"

The remainder of the day dragged on with nothing to look forward to except a spectacular meal of stewed fish and beans, a huge cup of cocoa and another testicular wrap, inconsonant with what the good doctor had promised, that had to be secured with several traversals of scotch tape around my legs. Given the palatability of the food, I requested another serving but it never came.

After lunch, which I guessed was served promptly at noon, I longed for a novel but having none I entertained myself by casting evasive stares at the patients. I was still unaware of the date and had again lost track of time, however transient visitors had begun to intersperse with the nurses who were still as busy as bees, which meant it was probably four o'clock. Mr. Thomas had a female visitor whom he introduced, in a low whisper, as his wife. I waved at her. Mr. Deonarine had a company of ten who all addressed him as Daddy; it was strange to see mature children. *The man in a lot of pain* had a female visitor who spoke loudly about peanuts during her entire stay; I couldn't figure whether '*peanuts*' was the code for testicles or if the lady was a peddler of the sorts, regardless, her sentences ironically took the following forms: "my peanuts are better than yours," "but your peanuts are bigger," "your peanuts are always salty," and "your customers like your peanuts big." I guessed: *The man in a lot of pain* was a nuts-man and his visitor was a competitor.

My visitors were Gerard, Andy, Eva, Lisa and her husband, Ian. They looked displeased about my new location and during that time, a nurse brought a blood bag which she attached to a tube leading to Mr. Thomas' hand. Thick blood pulsated from the bag and flowed along the tube. With this, my visitors seemed anxious to leave and when the bell rang, they vamoosed.

Darkness approached slowly then fell suddenly, and with it came the screams.

I passed that night in solemn meditation. It occurred to me repeatedly that in my healthy life, away from this place, I probably enjoyed cheap pleasures while there were people who suffered. Additionally, I had invested so much time, effort and money in an attempt to lavishly decorate my room and purchase items yet to be enjoyed. What about the people who died and had just gotten married or purchased a new house? From the little I could see of the sky, I promised myself that I would never again live a life that was selfish and thoughtless. I prayed for forgiveness and trusted that God had heard me.

Eventually, I fell into a peaceful sleep.

A banshee's shriek woke me. I shot up, heavy with sweat, and scrutinised the black room: Mr. Alexander was asleep – his mouth opened in its usual look of amazement or silent scream – along with Mr. Thomas and Mr. Deonarine. A light flicked on, subduing yet amplifying my horror, and illuminated the area where *The man in a lot of pain* lay on all fours, like a quadruped. He wore a vest and diaper and in gut-wrenching anguish, he petitioned The Father, The Son and The Holy Spirit for mercy through death, and while this was not my first brush with suicide, it was unsettling to witness his ordeal. Suddenly, the same Asian doctor, clad in a pinafore made of garbage bags, the one who had applied my *tourniquet*, appeared at his bedside and importuned in what my unskilled ear identified as an exaggerated *Chinese accent*:

"Mista, can you tell me what wong? Mista, please tell me what wong with you. Mista what is wong with you? I can't help you if you don't tell me what wong, Mista! Mista, speak to me! You must tell me!"

Seconds later, after the patient had failed to respond, I sat up as the bleakness deepened, worried that he had died. Without warning he howled, as if about to transform into a werewolf, and, as if a dam had burst, blood gushed from an unidentified *somewhere* and an impasto of red flooded his bed and the floor. I gasped in horror and it occurred to me that I had walked past that very spot; this abject memory haunts me whenever I walk barefooted, particularly on a refined or polished green surface.

The Asian doctor complained sharply:

"Mista, look what you doing! You are messing up the place! Please tell me what is wong with you!"

He gesticulated wildly, his moves and the *tourniquet* he had administered to my genitals, convincing me that he was only a fledgling. I vanquished my observation, rotating to my right, suddenly aware of the pool of sweat in which I lay and facing the *still* sleeping Mr. Thomas and the world beyond the windows. Then, overwhelmed by the anxiety to return home and the fallacious impression that I had been warded weeks ago, I stuck my index fingers into my ears and cried until the sun elevated in the east.

I yearned for a bath before breakfast but vowed that I

wouldn't walk past the glossy floor from which the pool of blood had been swiped clean. Even the linen on which *The man in a lot of pain* lay was a dazzling white, and his languid demeanour and crossed legs advocated that the events of the previous night might have been a transient dream. Perplexed by this thought, I rummaged through the bag which Lisa had hand-delivered on her last visit. In it was a mule two sizes too small for size eleven feet, but at least it promised to protect my toes and heels from the floor. I hustled them on, skirted *The man in a lot of pain* and headed to the bathroom where I indulged in a long, hot shower.

Refreshed, I returned to see a group of unfamiliar nurses along with a stout Chinese doctor, gathered around Mr. Thomas; the curtain was opened so I saw and heard them clearly. The doctor, because of his brutal frankness, was the best yet worst kind. He said:

"Mr. Thomas, if you do not get the other pints of blood you will die very soon. Who knows, maybe by Monday, but in the meantime we *must* discharge you since there is nothing we can do for you without the blood."

My heart bled for Mr. Thomas who was two shy of the quantum of five pints, and who cried in uncertainty as this final dictum was delivered. The doctor signed a surfeit of documents then wobbled over to my bedside with his flock in tow. He had a fat, cerise face, which women had probably pinched to pulp as a kid, and a large, black pouch strapped around his waist as if he were a tourist. His first words, although robotic and stony, were glorious to my ears.

"You, my friend," he said slowly, flipping through my

records in a manner which suggested grievous news, "…
you will be discharged today. Of course you will come
back for a clinical appointment sometime soon and we
will see if you might need surgery, but in the meantime
you will be treated with antibiotics for an infection."

He flashed a grand smile as if just as happy as I
was. Maybe it was because my departure meant one less
patient, I assumed stupidly, but now I strongly believe
that he, along with the others who had attended to me,
truly cared. With a wagging forefinger, tilted head and
elevated brows, he concluded:

"If you come back and need surgery we will stitch
those two balls of yours to the wall of your scrotum.
When we are done you can do the twist, but your testicles?
Oh-no-no-no-no-no! They cannot do the twist."

He alone chortled at his joke, which struck me as
rehearsed and abused, then he left with his reticent
disciples to attend to Mr. Alexander who, at the pat of
his head, howled:

"Oh-gawd-oh-gawd-oh-gawd-oh-gawd!"

Home time, please

◇◇

Lisa arrived at Ward Twenty-one twelve o'clock sharp. I was already armed with my discharge form, a prescription and hot cocoa in my stomach, lying, thinking how promising the day seemed. With my tiny slippers on my feet and bags of dirty linen in my hands, I waved a silent goodbye to the patients who had become my brothers in pain and all but the doddering Mr. Alexander responded. With pressing adjustments to my testicles, I stumbled past nurses, doctors and other patients, thanking the staff and wishing best of luck to the visitors.

Outside, an infantile artist had smudged the sky grey and it abruptly began drizzling, but Lisa The Meticulous was ready; she fussed open an umbrella large enough for one and as I had just been discharged, through tacit agreement I became priority while my sister vainly shielded her head with slender fingers. We hobbled to the car and drove out of the hospital car park as a thick sheet of grey rain laundered Port of Spain.

Returning to Trincity was like coming from a traumatic journey that had been too long.

The house was more homely than I could recall. I hopped inside, hoping to evade any neighbours and well-wishers, and unlocked the side door to the small but magical washroom. I exhaled slowly; I was really home. A few twist and turns later, I stood enthralled before the closed door to my room. When I turned the knob the entry swung open slowly.

The anarchy I had left behind had vanished!

The walls were an impasto of orange and yellow. The new bed, although still wrapped in plastic, had been adorned in a comforter I had purchased months ago. The glass desk was in its assigned corner with a flat panel monitor perched atop it, looking greater than I had ever envisioned.

My jaw drooped and my spermatic cord knotted, prompting me to flop into the bed which felt perfect.

Minutes later, I slumbered, my *two* testicles intact. And in sack.